S0-FAF-864

WITHDRAWN
HARVARD LIBRARY
WITHDRAWN

Dumont on Religion

Key Thinkers in the Study of Religion

Edited by Steven Engler, Mount Royal College, Canada

Key Thinkers in the Study of Religion is a series of compact introductions to the life and work of major figures in the study of religion. Each volume provides up-to-date critical evaluations of the place and value of a single scholar's work, in a manner both accessible to students and useful for instructors. Each volume includes a brief biography, analyses of key works, evaluations of criticisms and of overall impact on the field, and discussions of the work of later scholars who have appropriated or extended each key thinker's approach. Critical engagement with each key thinker's major works makes each volume a useful companion for the study of these important sources in the field. Aimed at the undergraduate and introductory graduate classrooms, the series aims to encapsulate and evaluate foundational contributions to the academic study of religion.

This series is sponsored by, supported by the North American Association for the Study of Religion (NAASR), an affiliate of the International Association for the History of Religions.

Published:

Bourdieu on Religion: Imposing Faith and Legitimacy
Terry Rey

Lévi-Strauss on Religion: The Structuring Mind
Paul-François Tremlett

Forthcoming:

Bastide on Religion: The Invention of Candomblé
Michel Despland

Derrida on Religion: Thinker of Differance
Dawne McCance

Rudolf Otto on Religion
Gregory D. Alles

Dumont on Religion:
Difference, Comparison, Transgression

Ivan Strenski

LONDON OAKVILLE

Published by Equinox Publishing Ltd.

UK: Unit 6, The Village, 101 Amies St.,London SW11 2JW
USA: DBBC, 28 Main Street, Oakville, CT 06779

www.equinoxpub.com

First published 2008

© Ivan Strenski 2008

All rights reserved. No part of this publication may be reproduced or transmitted in any form or by any means, electronic or mechanical, including photocopying, recording or any information storage or retrieval system, without prior permission in writing from the publishers.

British Library Cataloguing-in-Publication Data
A catalogue record for this book is available from the British Library.

Library of Congress Cataloging-in-Publication Data

Strenski, Ivan.
Dumont on religion: difference, comparison, transgression / Ivan Strenski.
    p. cm. — (Key thinkers in the study of religion)
Includes bibliographical references and index.
ISBN-13: 978-1-84553-273-4 (hb)
ISBN-13: 978-1-84553-274-1 (pbk.)
1. Religion. 2. Dumont, Louis, 1911–1998. I. Title. BL51.S77 2008
    200.92—dc22

                        2008001913

Edited and Typeset by Queenston Publishing, Hamilton, Canada

Printed and bound in Great Britain by Lightning Source UK, Ltd., Milton Keynes, and Lightning Source Inc., La Vergne, TN

Contents

Acknowledgments

Introduction

Chapter 1   What Can we Learn from Louis Dumont?   1

Chapter 2   A Contrarian's Most Contrarian Notion: 21
              Dumont on Hierarchy

Chapter 3   Our Individualism and Its Religious Origins   51

Chapter 4   The Comparative Risks of Comparison: 89
              On Not "Remaining Caged within Our Own
              Frame of Reference"

Chapter 5   Conclusion: Dumont's Morality and Social   119
              Cosmology

References   137
Index   143

In memory of

Dr. Philippe Besnard (1942–2003)

Directeur, Observatoire Sociologique du Changement,
Co-Founder, Groupe d'études durkheimiennes,
Directeur, Centre National de la Recherche Scientifique (CNRS)
Member, Groupe d'étude des méthodes de l'analyse sociologique (GEMS)
Editorial Committee, Directeur, *Revue française de sociologie*

On behalf of the many American scholars that you helped to
uncover the research treasures of Paris; in fond recollection
of your kindness, candor and support for our work; in thanks
for those priceless personal introductions to your colleagues
and associates; in gratitude for your generous reception of us
as colleagues; we thank you.

Acknowledgements

Louis Dumont and Suzanne Tardieu-Dumont, Justin McDaniel, Jean-Claude Galey, Bill Pickering, Joel Robbins, Ellen Strenski, The "Big Island" —Hawai'i, Bobi Moreno, Akiko Masuda, J-M. Vimala-Soprano, Elizabeth Collins, The Holstein Family and Community Endowment, Daniel De Coppet, Stanley Insler, Heinz Bechert, Claude Lévi-Strauss, Ninian Smart, The British Centre for Durkheimian Studies, and especially, Philippe Besnard, the staff and facilities of La Maison des Sciences de l'Homme.

Chapter One

What Can We Learn from Louis Dumont?

> During the 1960s, Lévi-Strauss was the most prestigious name in the domain of the human sciences. But, for me as for some others, the work of Dumont had been the most decisive.
>
> Tzvetan Todorov (Todorov 2002, 218)

By most conventional accounts, the chief contemporary presence of the study of religion begun by Durkheim and his immediate circle is Claude Lévi-Strauss. But while in the study of myth, ritual, totemism, or symbolism, Lévi-Strauss' name comes readily enough to mind, little else bearing *directly* on the study of religion can be attributed to the father of modern structuralism. Far more directly involved in the study of religion, but oddly enough far less appreciated despite being so, is the French structuralist Louis Dumont (1911–1998). Going even further beyond just the study of religion, historian Mark Lilla claims that "after Lévi-Strauss surely the most important anthropologist in postwar France was Louis Dumont" (Lilla 1999, 41). Despite what many may imagine, as far as structural studies of *religion* are concerned, true pride of place should probably be yielded to Dumont as someone generally overshadowed by Lévi-Strauss' brilliant reputation. As suggested by the recent critique of Lévi-Strauss by Maurice Godelier, at best, Levi-Strauss occupies an ambiguous position in religious studies (Godelier 1999, 21f). Given Lévi-Strauss' denial of scientific status to the Durkheimian category of sacred, "religious anthropology ... will lose its autonomy and its specific character" (Lévi-Strauss 1963, 104). Indeed, Lévi-Strauss charted a course through his career that withdrew more and more from the study of religion even though his first substantial academic appointment was explicitly in the study of religion at the École Pratique des Hautes Études. This career in upper reaches of the French academic world began by Lévi-Strauss succeeding the religious phenomenologist, Maurice Leenhardt, in the so-called "Marcel Mauss Chair" in the Religious Sciences (Fifth) Section of the Paris École Pratique des Hautes Etudes.

© Equinox Publishing Ltd. 2008, Unit 6, The Village, 101 Amies Street, London SW11 2JW

As soon as he was able, however, Lévi-Strauss withdrew further from institutionalized religious studies in France. In 1959, he took final leave of the institutional structures of the study of religion in France by quitting the Fifth Section for the College de France, where no disciplinary structures apply.

By contrast with Lévi-Strauss, Dumont's work has become increasingly involved in areas recognized as the domain of the study of religion. Thus, while most students of religion may only recall Dumont's classic study of the Hindu caste system, *Homo Hierarchicus* or his work on the institution of world renunciation in the religions of India, there is far more. This, of course is not to discount Dumont's achievements in the special area studies of the religions of India, where he ranks with distinguished figures such as Sylvain Lévi, Louis Renou, or Paul Mus. But, it is to point out how much more Dumont has contributed to our understanding of religion than can be encompassed within his Indian anthropological studies. There is what I shall call the career of Dumont as humanist or moralist. Here, I seek to increase the awareness of students of religions of implications and explicit contribution of Dumont to our understanding of religious beliefs and institutions, ethics, ideology, values, world-views and such. Here, Dumont takes his place alongside congenial classic moralist authors such as Tocqueville, Durkheim, Mill and Weber, or moderns like Robert Bellah, Isaiah Berlin, Michel Foucault or Tzvetan Todorov. Here, we would need to include Dumont's work on individualism as our modern ideology, his epistemological work on category formation of such cultural *a prioris* as politics, economics and religion, his lifelong devotion to the comparative studies of civilizations, and the ethical implications of his work. My purpose in writing this book is precisely to raise the level of recognition among students of religions for Dumont's work in the humanistic and *moraliste* study of religion.

This volume is dedicated to bringing out how Dumont ranges farther afield from his own highly technical studies of marriage, filiation and kinship into studies with tremendous implications for the humanistic study of religion. A short list of these includes Dumont's investigations into the historical and philosophical foundations of Western individualist ideology and "Eastern" otherworldly withdrawal from society, his sociological meditations on the paradoxical roots of fascism, totalitarianism and modern-day racism, his out-of-season querying of our ideals of equity as exhausted by the notion of equality, our conviction of the objectivity and natural character of cultural aprioris such as economy, politics and religion, our prejudices favoring conflict models of society, and so on. This volume, therefore, seeks to show how and in what sense Dumont is a "Key Thinker" in the study of religion.

© Equinox Publishing Ltd. 2008

Focal themes: Hierarchy, individualism and comparison

Although Dumont tackles such a wide range of issues, when examined carefully, it is clear that they cluster around two dialectically opposed notions: hierarchy and the individual. Let us consider hierarchy first. Conveniently, Dumont's work here corresponds to the first phase of his intellectual career—his ethnographically-based writings on India. While Dumont's idea of hierarchy developed from his field-specific work in India, hierarchy for Dumont is a cross-culturally comparative notion of great application and power. It breaks out of the culturally-specific confines of the Indian context, and shapes the rest of Dumont's intellectual life.

In the 1960s, Dumont's *Homo Hierarchicus* attempted to account for the Hindu caste system in terms of his theoretical principle of hierarchy. In doing so however, Dumont roused the moral indignation of scholars offended by what they took to be an attack on egalitarian ideals of social justice. It also stirred the political pot among French intellectuals of the left. Many suspected Dumont of cryptically approving the inequities of tasks, perhaps ultimately wanting to legitimate systems of inequity in our own society. While Dumont denied defending schemes of degradation in India (untouchability), or in America (racism), doubts still lingered. In the United States, the anthropologist Gerald Berreman of the University of California at Berkeley, also joined the chorus condemning Dumont's apparent approval of systems of inequality. Were Dumont's critics correct, especially about his moral and political orientations? What really is the deep logic of Dumont's view of hierarchy? Was he really trying to foist upon the modern world an archaic system of hierarchy rooted in ancient times?

Conveniently as well, the second axis around which Dumont's intellectual life revolves—individualism—stands both for the dominant ideology of the West, and as the dialectical opposite of hierarchy. Marking the second phase of his intellectual career, in the 1970s, Dumont, in a way, turned his back on India and hierarchy and confronted Western individualism with that same sense of strangeness as typical of an anthropological "other." The studies of this second phase of Dumont's intellectual career traced the genesis of Western individualism from its beginnings in Christianity to its development in modern economic and political thought. Here, Dumont turned from the role of ethnographer to one of intellectual historian, from someone immersed in the participant observers role in an exotic faraway field to a student of primary and historical texts.

In its own paradoxical way, Dumont's approach to individualism only deepened his investigations into hierarchy. For Dumont to study individualism was to study hierarchy from its other side, so to speak. Studying India had been for him another way of studying ourselves; studying

© Equinox Publishing Ltd. 2008

ourselves, in turn, shed light upon all those civilizations utterly at odds with ours, India included. Hierarchy was basic Hindu caste society; individualism was fundamental to our liberal democratic society in the West. Hierarchy and individualism therefore are posed as two principles dialectically opposite but internally connected. We learned about ourselves by posing us over against the other.

For Dumont, one of the problems with previous studies of individualism was the fact that it was conceived abstractly by investigators. The Enlightenment bears most of the responsibility for such an approach, since it conceived the human individual apart from its social relations, and exalted in the fact of such liberation. But Dumont wants to change this by conceiving the individual as incorporating the social dimension of human life. In short, he argues that although we have tended to see individualism as the utter negation of society and hierarchy, individualism might better be conceived—paradoxical as it may seem—as entailing hierarchy and including society. By this, he means that individualism is a product of the decision to rank—in effect, to hierarchize. The individual is placed over and above the group; the group is retained in "second place," as it were, on a lower level.

This notion of individualism is particularly timely in light of the serious struggles now underway to decide how democratic values might be understood in such diverse contexts as the Muslim revival or in the post-communist Europe. These cultures, many with strong holistic and religious social traditions, are still seeking how to comprehend individualism in a way consonant both with their traditional religious values and their new secular aims. They desire to conceive the individual in a way which cherishes the rights essential to democratic society, but without losing sight of the collective and holistic values of community. How could one conceive the individual in such environments without at the same time simply repeating the course taken by the European Enlightenment and Reformation—two movements that have, on the whole, found it difficult to accommodate the social dimensions of being human. But these new late emerging nations and societies are eager to accommodate social life to the life of the individual. Therefore, a hierarchical construction of individualism might provide the conceptual leverage needed for this synthesis, since it includes society as integral to the individual.

Before we get on with the principal business of this treatment of Louis Dumont, let me sketch major points of his life and works.

Biographical sketch: Louis Dumont (1911–1998)

Louis Dumont was born in the Ottoman city of Salonika, Turkey in 1911,

© Equinox Publishing Ltd. 2008

where his father had been an engineer in the service of the Turkish government. In the early 1930s, he began studies in mathematics at the École Polytechnique in Paris. But, he soon became alienated from his studies and in what he refers to as a fit of "youthful rebellion," Dumont abandoned his program at the EP and enjoyed something of a bohemian life in Paris, where he met members of the Collège de Sociologie, most important of all, Roger Caillois. Because of his decision to abandon his studies, Dumont was virtually disowned by his family—his mother was by then a widow. His defiance of parental wishes cast him out into the world, where he had to make his own living. After some time indulging in the pleasures of the city, in 1936 Dumont began to attend lectures by Marcel Mauss at the Institut d'Ethnologie. This encounter proved to be pivotal in moving him to become an anthropologist. Here as well began Dumont's considerable interests in India, since his teacher, Marcel Mauss, commanded this special area of expertise. In order to support himself during this period and until the late 1930s Dumont did clerical work at the Musée National des Arts et Traditions Populaires. Later this institution was to give birth to the Musée de l'Homme.

In 1939, Dumont volunteered for military service, but was captured by the Germans at the end of the so-called "Phony War" (drôle de guerre) in Spring 1940. Just before the war, Dumont would marry his first wife, Simone. She was to help him through the difficult years to follow by sending him books to read while he was imprisoned in Germany. Simone also accompanied Dumont on his field trips to India. During the time of his imprisonment in Germany, near Hamburg, Dumont learned German and later Sanskrit from the Jaina specialist, Professor Walther Schubring (University of Hamburg). With the connivance of friendly prison guards, he was able to absent himself in the evenings after his assigned factory work.

From May 1945, Dumont returned to the Musée National des Arts et Traditions Populaire, specializing on antique French furniture. Encouraged both by the great Indo-Europeanist, Professor Georges Dumézil, and the director of Musée National des Arts et Traditions Populaire, Georges-Henri Rivière, Dumont began field studies in the Provencal town of Tarascon of a festival of the Rhône River monster, "La Tarasque." These studies bore fruit in the 1951 publication of Dumont's first original monograph, *La Tarasque*.

In 1948, Dumont left on his first years of fieldwork in India, armed with the new structural methods he had learned from Lévi-Strauss. The two anthropologists had met briefly in 1936, and then, after a gap of 12 years, were reunited at the Musée National des Arts et Traditions Populaire. Taking Lévi-Strauss' structural ideas into the field, Dumont pursued his studies in the south of India from late 1948 to 1950 in Pramalai Kallar and

© Equinox Publishing Ltd. 2008

Tamilnadu. The results this combination of structural method and intense empirical research in India resulted in the publication in 1975 of *Une Sous-caste de l'Inde du Sud*, and earlier, as we will note of Dumont's great classic on caste in India, *Homo Hierarchicus* (1967).

From 1951–1955, Dumont moved to England where he took up a post of lecturer at the Institute of Anthropology in Oxford. Dumont tells us that his close working relation with Professor E.E. Evans-Pritchard there gave him special insights into the British anthroplogical world, and in particular to its Durkheimian clientele there, Mary Douglas and A.R. Radcliffe-Brown. Before returning to Paris after his sojourn in Oxford, Dumont returned to India in 1955 for a further 6 months of fieldwork in north India. In 1957–1958, Dumont did an additional 15 months of fieldwork in north India—in Gorakhpur

Between these fieldwork trips in 1955, Dumont assumed the post of Director d'Études at the École Pratique des Hautes Études, VIième Section, a division of the EPHE associated primarily with historians of the *Annales* School, such as Ferdinand Braudel. Dumont set to work immediately to establish the Centre d'Études indienne, and before leaving again for India in 1957, he collaborated with British anthropologist, David Pocock, in founding the periodical *Contributions to Indian Sociology*. In 1975, when the EPHE, VIth split into groupings of historians, on the one side, and social scientists on the other, Dumont would follow other social scientists in the formation of the École des Hautes Études en Sciences Sociales.

From the early 1960s, Dumont began a series of publications on caste, individualism and world renunciation in Indian religion, among them his *La Civilisation indienne et nous* (1964) The publication of Dumont's great work on caste, *Homo Hierarchicus*, in 1965, marked a kind of high-water mark of his Indological work. His essays on world-renunciation in India would be gathered into an anthology in 1970—*Religion/Politics and History in India*.

From the middle 1960s onward, Dumont's work took a turn toward a critical intellectual history of the main ideology of the West—individualism. The first essay on individualist ideology in the West appeared in 1965, and in 1977, his first book in a series on individualist ideology in the West was published, *Homo Aequalis I: genèse et épanouissement de l'idéologie économique—From Mandeville to Marx* (English edition). By 1982, Dumont was ready to make his strongest statement concerning the religious origins of the Western ideology of individualism, which appeared in the journal, *Religion*, "A Modified View of Our Origins: the Christian Beginnings of Modern Individualism." Then shortly thererafter, he collected his shorter writings on individualism into his *Essais sur l'individualisme* (1983), later to appear in English translation as *Essays on Individualism* (1986) In 1991, the second and final volume of Dumont's work on individualism in the West was published—*Homo Aequalis II: L'idéologie*

© Equinox Publishing Ltd. 2008

allemande: France–Allemagne et retour (English translation 1994, *German Ideology: From France to Germany and back.*

A life: The Big Picture

Dumont was born into a bourgeois French family, descendent from generations of artistic craftsmen. Partly as a result of the expectations of his family, Dumont was pressed to enter higher education in the scientific, technological or mathematical fields. Perhaps already reflecting a theoretical turn of mind, Dumont chose mathematics. In his early twenties, Dumont rebelled against the strictures of this rigorous and somewhat desiccated type of education, with its predictable and direct career path into industry or government. In an act of youthful rebellion, he abandoned the studies that might have promised him a tranquil career, and launched out into the unknown. As he tells it, he was hungry for a life of reckless nonconformity, even though it caused major pain for his family: "This act of brash transgression "provoked a veritable scandal. My mother [a widow at the time], who had made sacrifices so that I could graduate, showed me the door. I refused to work. I wanted to live!" (Bruckner 1992, 68). Reveling in the cultural and artistic excitement of Paris of the late 1920s and 1930s, Dumont worked at the best jobs he could get, menial though they might be, and indulged his interests in the feverish activities of the *avant-garde* aesthetic, philosophical and social group of the epoch. Of those years. In particular, in the early 1930s, Dumont spent some time on the fringes of cultural rebellion, associating with radical Surrealists poets, philosophers and political thinkers, who had affinities with such groups as Collège de Sociologie, of which Georges Bataille and Roger Caillois were members (Collins 1988).

Steven Collins and Roland Lardinois have delved deeper into Dumont's admission that as a young man he was influenced by René Guénon, the mystical and esotericist French writer of the early part of the last century. (Collins 1988; Lardinois 1996) Collins argues that Dumont was introduced to the thought of René Guénon by Roger Caillois, who at that time was a student of Marcel Mauss' as well as a significant figure in the literary avant-garde. René Guénon had converted to Islam in 1912, and allied himself with the Sufi tradition. The mystical nature of this Islamic tradition provided an easy transition for Guénon to begin his studies on India and other religions farther east. In 1921, he wrote a general introduction to the study of Hindu beliefs—*Introduction générale è l'étude des doctrines hindouse* as well as another book on Hindu philosophy translated as *Man and His Becoming according to the Vedanta* (1925). Like many other esotericist thinkers of his kind, Guénon saw Eastern thought as containing hidden or forgotten wisdom that had been pushed aside by the advance of rationalism and moder-

© Equinox Publishing Ltd. 2008

Roland Lardinois and the occultist genesis of Dumont's thought about India

Recently, French anthropologist, Roland Lardinois has made the controversial claim that Dumont's thought about India reflects the views of early twentieth-century mystic, René Guénon (Collins 1988; Lardinois 1996). Dumont is accused, in effect, of hiding his youthful enthusiasms for Guénon out of a sense of embarrassment. Since Dumont seems to have continued to use Guénonian ideas, his anthropology can no longer be considered "scientific." Furthermore, Guénon was a propagandist for the French right-wing. Lardinois insinuates that Dumont follows Guénon down the same right-wing path (Lardinois 1996).

Roman Catholic born Guénon converted to Islam in 1912, and was quickly drawn to Sufism. His tastes for Muslim mysticism then gave way to an interest in Indian mysticism. In Guénon's eyes the "East" was a font of forgotten wisdom, eagerly pushed aside by the West in our rush toward embracing individualism and egalitarianism. Like Dumont, Guénon's writings on caste relied on the idea of hierarchy (Collins 1988). Truth be told, Dumont was never aligned with the right-wing, but instead sits squarely in the middle of the political spectrum. Nor do Dumont's theoretical ideas originate in the mystico-occultist discourse of Guénon's very unscientific career.

Lardinois' critique of Dumont fails because there is no real "influence" of Guénon upon Dumont. While Dumont admitted his youthful attraction for Guénon, there is no real dependence of Dumont's theories upon Guénon. The major features of Dumont's thought that Lardinois tracks to Guénon, for example, could just as well be traced to another thinker—say, Marcel Mauss, Dumont's own teacher. Nor do the ideas of Dumont's that Lardinois identifies as due to Guénon require some kind of grounding in Guénon's world view. They make sense in their own terms within the argumentative framework supplied by Dumont.

nity. The prime culprit in this loss of traditional wisdom was the dominance of individualism and egalitarianism in the West. Guénon also wrote on the caste system, and opposed the principle of hierarchy found there diametrically to the egalitarian individualism of the West (Collins 1988).

Since the question may arise to readers, it would be well to note that some contemporary critics of Dumont's, such as Roland Lardinois, claim that Dumont has minimized the depths of his youthful enthusiasms for Guénon. Lardinois claims that Dumont has done so partly to defend the scientific character of an anthropology that shares so many fundamental

© Equinox Publishing Ltd. 2008

values with the foggy old mystic. How, Lardinois in effect asks, can we take seriously the scientific character of Dumont's thought when we find that many of its fundamental orientations originate in the thinking of such a discredited figure as Guénon? Further, Lardinois implies, is not a powerful reason for Dumont's playing down of his intellectual debts to Guénon a secret desire stealthily to promote today the same anti-modern values that Guénon championed years ago (Lardinois 1996)?

This may not be the place to address all these points in detail, since we will take them up in a later chapter. Suffice it to say that Dumont has made no secret of his liberal, but skeptical, political affections, although they are hard to label in the simplistic terms of the political discourse today. On the one side, contemporary "French" intellectuals such as Tzvetan Todorov, Luc Ferry or Alain Finkielkraut cite Dumont with admiration. Like members of the so-called "Nouvelles Philosophes," Dumont has made his preferences clear for the likes of pragmatic social democrats like Marcel Mauss, Roger Caillois, Max Weber, and Raymond Aron. In personal comments to me, Dumont said with a tacit admission of past misjudgments that France "owed a lot" to De Gaulle. On the other side, Dumont has privately and by implication expressed contempt for the establishment "left" in France, in his day, so powerful and fashionable a voice among French intellectuals. Sartre, Althusser and even Lévi-Strauss have stirred Dumont to angry comments for their totalitarian willingness to sacrifice all other social values to that of those espoused by the "totalitarian" left. In particular, Dumont felt that an unqualified promotion of equality at the expense of other values, such as liberty or fraternity, would be a disaster for French democracy. Giving voice to his critical opposition to regimes that have tried to pass as marxist, Dumont sarcastically remarked in the early 1980s that

> in the politico-economic domain, France has outrageously underestimated India in relation to China, finding the Maoist promotion of equality, even as it suppressed "liberty" and undermined "fraternity" in the form of free association, for example, morally superior to an India in which bourgeois liberty flourished, but amid rigid and brutal economic inequality. On the one hand, people on the fashionable left swallowed everything about Maoist China, including the horrors of the "Cultural Revolution." Yet, in India they saw nothing but a combination of a decadent post-colonial bourgeois country married to the hideous cruelties of the Hindu caste system. Mrs. Gandhi's authoritarian rule was decried, while Maoist democracy was envied.

(Delacampagne 1981, 5)

Dumont here expresses at the same time skepticism to faith expressed by these lions of the French left that society would, on the whole, be a better if we were to suppress liberty and fraternity to equality. Dumont in part is skeptical about the program of the radical egalitarians because

© Equinox Publishing Ltd. 2008

they equate the ideal of justice—fairness or equity—with equality. We will take up this point in our discussion of hierarchy, for there, Dumont implies that systems of justice may be more complicated and thus differentiated than radical egalitarians admit. In this, Dumont is closer to the values expressed in Marx' slogan from the *Critique of the Gotha Program*, "From each according to his abilities to each according to his needs." There, Marx announces that fairness and equality are not the same thing each person does not necessarily receive an equal amount of goods or services as another. Women may be especially sensitive to this perspective in their often unhappy experience of public restroom facilities. Both men's and women's facilities may provide an *equal* number of restrooms or toilet units, but given the different anatomies of men and women, the result— to be observed during the intermission at any large public event when women queue up impatiently outside their restrooms—is gross unfairness to women. To make the situation fair or equitable, such public spaces should vastly increase the number of facilities for women: calculated *inequality* would make conditions fair for women, while equality fails to do them justice.

The upshot of this and other political interpretations of Dumont's thinking is that although Lardinois is undoubtedly correct in implying that Dumont is no man of the left—at least not of the farther ends of the French left political inclination (which would be Stalinist, in any event)—he is not necessarily the kind of romantic rightist that Guénon was, trying to further a traditionalist, rightist agenda in modern France. His association with the likes of Todorov and the centrists of the Gaullist party mentioned already, suggests as much. On personal note, had Dumont been the kind of rightist that one might associate with Guénon, then it would be hard to explain why Dumont's first wife, alive through World War II in France, was a Jew of the Marais. French Gentile extreme rightist anti-traditionalists of the 1930s and 1940s, like Guénon, did not marry Jews, as did Dumont.

If Dumont's precise location on the French political spectrum may be put aside for a while, what, however, can one make of the implication of the epistemological point raised by Lardinois and Collins that the scientific status of Dumont's work is compromised by its apparent debt to a set of guiding ideas and orientations peculiar to Guénon? Lardinois believes that in Guénon's thought he has discovered the "unity of principles which underlie Dumont's anthropology" (Lardinois 1996, 27). This is to say that Dumont's *theoretical ideas*, his models and such originate in the mystico-occultist discourse of Guénon's very unscientific career. These would include Guénon's comparativism, especially as it posed West versus India as dichotomies corresponding to modernity over against tradition, individualism versus hierarchy, the principle of power versus that of influence as expressed in particular in the opposition of Kṣatriya to Brāhmin.

© Equinox Publishing Ltd. 2008

The main problem with Lardinois' critique is its many points of igno-rance. I shall point out but two, one his ignorance of the history of science, especially the history of how theories come to be, two, his ignorance of the logic of "influence."

First, historians of science, such as Paul Feyerabend and others, have argued that the *origins* of a scientist's theoretical ideas are irrelevant to their scientific status. Science is one thing, its inspirational models or images, another. Consider the case of the origins of a scientific notion, such as the Big Bang. It is well established that the originator of this theoretical idea, Father Georges Lemaitre, a Roman Catholic priest, modeled his con-cept of the "Big Bang" from biblical imagery of creation *ex nihilo*. Not only that, Lemaitre may well have been religiously—apologetically— motivated to propose the theory of the Big Bang *because* of his religious belief in creation *ex nihilo*. Thus, the theoretical idea of the Big Bang *originated* in a plainly unscientific tenet of religious faith—the Christian dogma that the universe came about at one go from a single moment by virtue of the will of God.

Consistency would then demand that Lardinois conclude that the Big Bang theory is not properly *scientific* because of its religious origins. But since neither Lardinois nor most other scholars interested in science would be prepared to say so, Lardinois would have to alter his implied and explicit attempts to minimize the scientific status of Dumont's anthropol-ogy. It simply does not matter where theoretical ideas *come from*. What matters—for a Lemaitre or a Dumont—is whether, when operationalized, they meet the standards of scientific scrutiny. Tellingly, what characterizes Dumont's work as much as his particular theoretical ideas is the sometimes mind-numbingly detailed empirical quality of his publications. Dumont's first monograph, *La Tarasque*, (1951) was devoted to a painstakingly detailed ethnographic study of a Provencal village festival at Tarascon, an ancient settlement along the Rhône River in the south of France. The fes-tival celebrated the miraculous acts of St. Martha in protecting its people from a marauding monster by employing charms and spells. Readers will note how Dumont describes his first book (1951) on the Tarasque—nota-bly early in his career when the influence of Guénon should have been at its height: "It is a funny book, a kind of excessively descriptive 'index card' that ought never to have been published had it not been for the fancy of Jean Paulhan" (Delacampagne 1984, 204).

Second is the matter of the much misunderstood notion of "influence." What would it mean to say, as Lardinois does, that Dumont was influenced by René Guénon? Presumably, the claim is about something significant and lasting, not just a superficial matter, not just a trace element of the thought of one person in the thinking of another. If it comes to such a sig-nificant matter, and thus if one wishes to credit someone as an "influence,"

© Equinox Publishing Ltd. 2008

Robert Alun Jones has argued that at least two criteria must be met. First, there needs to be awareness of this supposed "influence," and second, real dependence upon the thought of the "influence." (Jones 1977, 293) In our case, I think Lardinois' claims fail to carry much weight. For instance, while Dumont makes no secret of his youthful attraction for Guénon's thought, and is thus "aware" of the influence of the mystic in his thinking, can we say that there is "real dependence" of Dumont's arguments upon Guénon? Could the major features of Dumont's thought that Lardinois tracks to Guénon, for example, be traced to another thinker? Do the ideas of Dumont's that Lardinois identifies as due to Guénon *require* some kind of grounding in Guénon's world view? Or, do they make sense on their own within the argumentative framework supplied by Dumont?

I shall argue that while Guénon was an early stimulant to Dumont's thinking, not only do Dumont's ideas have a logic of their own within his own framework of thinking, but there were other thinkers, close to Dumont as well, who thought in ways that superficially resembled Guénon. This, as I shall now discuss, can be traced to an influence far more important to Dumont's intellectual formation than Guénon—Marcel Mauss.

At a glance:

Roland Lardinois and the occultist genesis of Dumont's thought about India

Roland Lardinois has recently argued that Dumont's mature thinking about India is indelibly indebted to the mystic, of René Guénon.

- This association allegedly undermines the scientific character of Dumont's thought.
- Guénon saw Western individualism and egalitarianism as responsible for Western cultural malaise.
- Guénon wrote as well on caste, and invoked hierarchy as a social principle diametrically opposed to the egalitarian individualism of the West.
- Dumont has made no secret of his one time youthful infatuation with Guénon.
- Yet, his political affiliations have been and are far from Guénon's.
- Moreover, Dumont's theoretical ideas do not originate in the mystico-occultist discourse of Guénon's very unscientific career, but with Marcel Mauss and other members of the Durkheimian circle, such as Céléstin Bouglé, author of *Essai sur le régime des castes*.

© Equinox Publishing Ltd. 2008

Dumont and Marcel Mauss

Although Guénon played a part in stimulating an interest in the impressionable young rebellious mind of Dumont in his early twenties, it was Marcel Mauss and the Durkheimian circle who really seem to have defined what was to be Dumont's approach to the sociology of India. Dumont's connections with the Durkheimians began in 1936, at the tender age of twenty-five. As luck would have it, besides being France's leading ethnologist, Mauss was an accomplished Indologist, having studied Sanskrit and the religions of India under the eminent Sylvain Lévi. In meeting Mauss and certain members of the Durkheimian circle, Dumont seems to have ended his youthful meanderings in the world of the avant-garde. One of the original members of Durkheim's original team, Céléstin Bouglé, had already written an important study of caste in India from a deliberately Durkheimian point of view in 1908, and reprised in a second edition in 1927—*Essais sur le régime des castes* (Bouglé 1908 [1927]). From Bouglé as well comes the very Dumontian-sounding *Les Idées égalitaires: étude sociologique* in 1899 (Bouglé 1899). So, both the themes of caste and individualism were well established parts of the Durkheimian repertoire of interests. Dumont, in brief, did not require Guénon's interest in the same themes to sustain his own.

Furthermore, as far as the style of scholarship practiced by Dumont's mentor, Marcel Mauss, a closer look at it and its genesis should go some way in dispelling how far Dumont was still in thrall to Guénon by the late 1930s when he began assembling the professional credentials of an ethnographer. Mauss' formation, for example, so critical to Dumont's own intellectual formation was not at all in the Guénonian mode. It drew in large part from the great French Indologist, Sylvain Lévi, who imposed upon Mauss a strict discipline for attending to and marshaling facts. Now, although Sylvain Lévi died in 1935, a year or so before Dumont began studying with Marcel Mauss, Lévi had already shaped Mauss to be a rigorously empirical scholar, who would be inclined to produce highly detailed, documentary style of French ethnography and history.

It was in this period of study under Mauss—1936 to be exact—that Dumont earned a living doing clerical work at the Musée des Arts et Traditions Populaire. He relates how it was under these circumstances that he first met Lévi-Strauss who had just returned from the field work in Brazil about which he wrote in his *Tristes tropiques*. Dumont's task was the menial one of typing up Lévi-Strauss's field notes before Lévi-Strauss's return to his post at the University of Sao Paolo.

If some element of rivalry, however subtle and civil, is to be noted between Dumont and Lévi-Strauss it may have to do with the disparity in

© Equinox Publishing Ltd. 2008

their social stations, but more likely because of the somewhat unscrupulous use Lévi-Strauss made of the reputation of Mauss to enhance his own in later years. (Lévi-Strauss 1967, 1987; Strenski 1985). The most emphatic intervention that Dumont made into this matter was the special point he made in calling attention to Mauss as a rigorous empiricist, largely to counter the impression that Lévi-Strauss had tried to create of Mauss as primarily a theorist. In truth, Lévi-Strauss never studied with Mauss (he only claimed to have met him once or twice). For Lévi-Strauss to have made of Mauss a precursor of his own theoretically high-flying structuralism was at best a distortion of who Mauss was and of what his scholarship really was like (Dumont 1986b). At any rate, we can see how deeply Mauss made his mark on Dumont from evidence such as Dumont's first book, *La Tarasque* (1951), as well as from the fact that Dumont immersed himself in intense language study, as well as several years of fieldwork in India. This marks Dumont not as the spiritual heir of Guénon the mystic, rapt in meditation and immured in his cell, but a true intellectual son of Marcel Mauss and the Durkheimian tradition of the scientific study of human societies and civilizations.

Dumont's studies with Mauss were interrupted by the mobilization for World War II. By the time the war had commenced, Dumont had not yet decided upon India as his special field of study. Almost immediately upon France's entering the war, Dumont and many others were taken prisoner after a German offensive brought an end to the *drôle de guerre* or so-called Phony War. He tells us that he first busied himself learning German and then, for no specific reason, took up with Sanskrit. Dumont was not released from prison until 1945, but during those six years of imprisonment, he managed to make the best of his time. His assignment was factory work in the suburbs of Hamburg. In the evenings he studied Sanskrit, using books that his wife had sent to him from France. In one of the absurdities that often attend warfare, thanks to the "connivance of a sentry" who kept guard over the French POWs, Dumont managed to slip "off the reservation" to study Sanskrit with the Jain specialist, Professor Walther Schubring. Later, Dumont got what amounted to "day release" from incarceration to continue work on his Sanskrit formally at the University of Hamburg for a good portion of his imprisonment during the war (Madan 1999, 475). In subsequent years, Dumont would apply himself to further language study, in particular of modern Hindi and Tamil.

In 1945, with the liberation of France, Dumont gained release after six years in captivity. One of his stronger resolves was to continue with the work he had begun in learning Sanskrit, and to then commence with his studies of India. But economic necessity intervened, and Dumont took a humble curatorial position with some research duties at the Musée des

© Equinox Publishing Ltd. 2008

Arts et Traditions Populaire—all the while completing his higher degree in ethnography. This institution was devoted to the material culture of France; the furniture collection was, for example, of special interest to Dumont, and the study of it was part of his curatorial assignment as was his mission to Tarascon to observe the exotic ritual of St. Martha and the dragon, held there annually. We can perhaps better understand how the fine-grained descriptive ethnography learned from Mauss in the 1930s was reinforced by the ethos of the Musée and applied to Dumont's work on ritual life in Tarascon in terms (Delacampagne 1981, 4). He completed writing *La Tarasque* there in about 1948, and by then, Dumont was ready for India. Thanks to the sponsorship of the great Indologist, Louis Renou, he was able to arrange a two year fieldwork trip to South India among his beloved Tamils.

It was during those somewhat lowly years at the Musée, that Dumont met Lévi-Strauss again. He and Dumont had first met in 1936, when Lévi-Strauss had first returned from his fieldwork in Brazil. Now, Lévi-Strauss had returned from his World War II exile in the Americas, ready to re-enter French academic life. Benefitting from the connections he had established before and through the war, Lévi-Strauss soon assumed a prestigious post at the École Pratique des Hautes Études, Fifth Section—ironically (and uncomfortably) as successor to the religious phenomenologist, Marcel Mauss' student, Maurice Leenhardt. I say "uncomfortably" because the Fifth Section was devoted to the study of religions, especially religious *texts*. Lévi-Strauss had little appetite either for religion or the study of texts, and left the École Pratique des Hautes Études at virtually the first opportunity for an—admittedly—"plum" appointment at the Collège de France. Despite their differences in social status, Lévi-Strauss readily shared his latest breakthrough work with Dumont, even to the extent of giving him advance copies of his great work on kinship, *The Elementary Structures of Kinship*. Dumont caught the structuralism "bug" instantly, especially for the way it helped him unlock some of the mysteries of kinship relations upon which he was intending to work in India. "The introduction of the idea of structure is the major event of our times in social anthropology and sociology," said Dumont in his masterpiece on the Hindu caste system, *Homo Hierarchicus* (Dumont 1980, 41). Thanks, then, to the generosity of Lévi-Strauss, and to the appeal of his theoretical vision, Dumont became a structuralist himself, although in a way that reflected all we have noted about Dumont's empiricist and documentary inclinations. We will also see that Dumont's application of his understanding of the structuralist program to studies of ideology, and thus in religion, likewise distinguish him from Lévi-Strauss (Dumont 1979a, 786).

By 1950, now nearing 40 years of age, Dumont's relentless effort to prepare himself for the profession finally bore fruit in an appointment to his

© Equinox Publishing Ltd. 2008

first academic job as Lecturer in social anthropology at Oxford. In those days, the department was chaired by the eminent E.E. Evans-Pritchard. That Evans-Pritchard extended the invitation to Dumont may be significant for at least two reasons. While he may be most widely known for his publications about the Nuer of East Africa, Evans-Pritchard was a great promoter of both the anthropological study of religion but also of the French—Durkheimian—School of sociology and social anthropology. One will do well to recall that Evans-Pritchard was something of an iconoclast because he pressed for a non-reductionist study of religion when so much of the work then being done cast religion as something to be "explained away" (Evans-Pritchard 1962). Moreover, Evans-Pritchard (and along with him, his colleague at Oxford, A.R. Radcliffe-Brown) had led the infiltration of Durkheimian approaches to the study of society into Britain. In Dumont, therefore, Evans-Pritchard might have imagined that he found an authentic real "blood line" heir of the Durkheimian tradition, as indeed he did. And, although Dumont might not have shown evidence of it at the time, Evans-Pritchard might have thought that he had also found someone sympathetic to his own advocacy of the study of religion. And, as we will see, he found that as well.

In 1955, Dumont returned to France and assumed a post in the "Section" of the École Pratique des Hautes Études (VIième) that had been devoted to history. Here is where the innovative historians of the *Annales* tradition held forth, such as Marc Bloch and Lucien Febvre—both profoundly and self-consciously committed to bringing the Durkheimian tradition's sociological and comparative perspectives to bear on history writing. The Durkheimians also influenced the *Annalistes* in adopting a style of doing history in the manner of ethnography. They, therefore, sought to give voice to the "folk" rather than the elites; they wrote about ritual and (often religious) folk traditions rather than the works of great literature. Like the Dumont of *La Tarasque* and furniture studies at the Musée des Arts et Traditions Populaire (and less like the Durkheimians) *Les Annalistes* were enthusiastic devotees to the study of material culture. Dumont, the historically attuned ethnographer, was a fine fit for historians who were attuned to ethnography. In a way, Dumont was to shift his membership from VIième Section, as it split into a Section for historians, proper, and another for social scientists —École des Hautes Études en Sciences Sociales. Dumont was to remain with the social scientists for rest of his days (Delacampagne 1981, 5).

Once Dumont had established himself with a steady income and a suitable institutional setting free exclusively to pursue writing and research, he put forth a stream of major publications for which he has become world famous. Since we will be discussing some of these in individual chapters,

© Equinox Publishing Ltd. 2008

I shall discuss only briefly Dumont's major works at this point, ranging from 1966 until a few years before Dumont's death in 1998.

First, are Dumont's most influential works arising out of his studies of India. On the side of "holism," so to speak, is his classic on the Indian caste system, *Homo Hierarchicus* (1966). On the side of the individual, *Religion/Politics and History in India* (1970) appeared deliberately to coincide with the publication in the same year as *Homo Hierarchicus*. This anthology collected a series of Dumont's essays all originally published in English, in part to be accessible to an Indian reading public. Here, Dumont assembled essays on subjects related to the notion of individualism, such as our Western way of looking at the world though individualist eyes, or on the nature of religious individualism—the renouncer tradition—in India. The overall effect was to place these two books into a thought-provoking dialectical relationship. From the middle 1970s, Dumont turned towards an examination of Western ideology. His first foray into this domain stood his Indian efforts on their head, so to speak: instead of hierarchy, Dumont focused on our Western ideology of equality. The key work here is *From Mandeville to Marx: The Genesis and Triumph of Economic Ideology* (1977), entitled tellingly in French as *Homo Aequalis* (1977). A complementary collection of studies explored the thought of German contributions to the idea of the individual. In its English edition, it was entitled *German Ideology: From France to Germany and Back* (1994). Significantly as well, in the French version, its title read *Homo Aequalis II*. Sandwiched in midway between these two treatments of equality was an anthology of essays published over the years on the genesis of the idea of the individual in the West, *Essays on Individualism: Modern Ideology in Anthropological Perspective* (1986 [1986a]). In the chapters to follow, we shall draw primarily from these major works.

What Dumont can teach us—among other things—about how to study religion?

If I were to try to conclude and summarize what I think the bottom-line value in the thought of Louis Dumont is, I think I would tend to dwell on certain broad intellectual attitudes, rather than any narrowly defined set of methodological principles.

1.We learn about ourselves by understanding others

While Dumont believes that individual cultures and civilizations have their own integrity, he nonetheless teaches us that we can better understand ourselves, and especially those deeply-embedded features of our way of looking on the world, by adopting a comparative perspective. India, for example, provides a mirror on the West. Studying traditional India, where

© Equinox Publishing Ltd. 2008

Biographical details at a glance: Louis Dumont (1911–1998)

- 1911, Louis Dumont born in Salonika.
- Early 1930s, he began studies in mathematics at the École Polytechnique in Paris.
- In 1936–1937, Dumont studied under Marcel Mauss.
- In 1939, Dumont volunteered for French army, but was made POW in Spring 1940.
- Spring 1940 to May 1945, Dumont interned as POW, but was able to receive instruction in Sanskrit from Professor Walther Schubring at the University of Hamburg.
- From May 1945, Dumont began field studies in the Provencal town of Tarascon of a festival of the Rhone River monster, "La Tarasque."
- In 1948, Dumont left on his first years of fieldwork in India.
- From late 1948 to 1950, Dumont pursued field studies in the south of India.
- In 1951, Dumont published his first monograph, *La Tarasque*.
- From 1951–1955, he lectured at the Institute of Anthropology in Oxford.
- In 1955, he returned to India for 6 months of fieldwork in north India.
- In 1955, Dumont assumed the post of Director d'Études at the École Pratique des Hautes Études, VIième Section.
- In 1957, in collaboration with British anthropologist, David Pocock, Dumont founded the periodical *Contributions to Indian Sociology*.
- In 1957–1958, Dumont did an additional 15 months of fieldwork in north India.
- From the early 1960s, Dumont began a series of publications on caste, individualism and world renunciation in Indian religion, among them his *La Civilisation indienne et nous* (1964).
- In 1965, Dumont's first essay on individualist ideology in the West appeared.
- In 1967, *Homo Hierarchicus*, Dumont's great work on caste was published.
- In 1975, Dumont would join in the formation of the École des Hautes Études en Sciences Sociales when it broke off from the Sixth Section. *Une Sous-caste de l'Inde du Sud* was also published in this year.
- In 1977, Dumont's first book in a series on individualist ideology in the West was published, *From Mandeville to Marx* (English edition).

© Equinox Publishing Ltd. 2008

Biographical details (continued)

- In 1982, Dumont's strongest statement concerning the religious origins of the Western ideology of individualism appeared in the journal, *Religion*, "A Modified View of Our Origins: the Christian Beginnings of Modern Individualism."
- In 1983, Dumont collected his shorter writings on individualism into his *Essais sur l'individualisme*, later to appear in English translation under as *Essays on Individualism* (1986).
- In 1991, the second volume of Dumont's work on individualism in the West was published—*Homo Aequalis II: L'idéologie allemande: France–Allemagne et retour* (English translation 1994), *German Ideology: From France to Germany and back.*

---

hierarchy explicitly dominates the traditional thought-world, forces us to think about how and where we, whom we think of as individualistic and thus anti-hierarchical, have hidden hierarchy in our own society.

2.What we don't know can hurt us

Some of our deeply-embedded culturally or civilizationally specific ideas are hidden to us—such as our own hidden assumptions of an individualist worldlier. Unless we become aware of these hidden assumptions and viewpoints, we will blind ourselves to others who arrange their worlds according to very different assumptions. Dumont believes, for example, that our prevailing individualism blinds us to different ways of organizing the world, such as hierarchy.

3.Ideas matter

While not dismissing material culture and the constraints it exerts on human behavior, Dumont teaches us that the way we think about things, the ideas and ideologies we have—whether hidden or not—make a difference to the way we act or behave. Our idea of the individual, for example, impinges upon the way we act toward one another, and most importantly for Dumont, upon the way we approach other cultures and civilizations (Dumont 1979a).

4.Cultures, civilizations are real

We should treat cultures and civilizations in the same way as we treat individuals, not as arbitrary mental constructs, but as beings that have their own lives and laws of operation.

5.Religions and ideologies ought to be studied as members of a common class

We should not shirk from studying such apparently different subjects

© Equinox Publishing Ltd. 2008

as, for example, individualist ideology and, say, Hinduism or Christianity because one is conventionally tagged an "ideology" and the other a "religion," but rather see both as expressions of encompassing values. As such, they may be related in many ways, say, as when Dumont tries to trace the genesis of individualism in Christianity, or perhaps to pose them as competing value systems in the modern world, when individualism is seen as a force which draws people away from care for each other.

6."Fear not to transgress": the contrarian's credo

One great moral lesson that the life and letters of Dumont may perhaps teach us is the value of risking to affront conventional wisdom. Dumont's notion of hierarchy, his critique of egalitarianism and so on may have led many to shun or misrepresent him. For this reason, some critics may claim that Dumont is neither the "Key Thinker" that this series aims to present, nor even that Dumont is important at all. Yet, Dumont's enduring fame and influence even beyond the special field of South Asian studies show that Dumont was on to something. His bravery in bringing such contrarian or taboo subjects to our attention is a mark of true virtue, of real intellectual courage, and one that I commend to all my readers. Part of what I hope to achieve in this book is to show in what sense we then can say that Dumont was a "Key Thinker" in the study of religion.

7.Ignoring religion as a factor in life only imposes a local value system

What Dumont learned in India was that the Western habit of ignoring religion as a factor in life was a deeply-rooted occidental prejudice. In order to understand many other societies successfully, we would need to liberate ourselves from this bias and consider the religious factors in social and cultural life. "The materialist perspective on society and history only furnishes a superficial contemporary viewpoint of a country such as India...." (Dumont 1964, 76).

© Equinox Publishing Ltd. 2008

Chapter Two

A Contrarian's Most Contrarian Notion: Dumont on Hierarchy

"Thou shalt neither think about hierarchy, nor with it"

"Joined at the hip" is the way we might describe Dumont's attachment to the concept of hierarchy. In one writing after another, Dumont has employed "hierarchy" as a key concept for understanding religion and society. More than that, Dumont has been forthright in his appreciation for the relative merits of religions and societies so organized, and eager to promote the insights gained thereby elsewhere. Many religious folk will tend to find the assertion of this notion congenial and perhaps long over-due. After all, to many religious folk, hierarchy can be an order ordained by the sacred, literally "the rule of the sacred (sometimes 'priest') —the '*archko*' of the '*hieros*'." Indeed, it might be seen as the essence of religion itself in proclaiming the governing role of the sacred. This would especially be true for most traditional religions, whether they be theistic, like Islam, Judaism or Christianity, or not, like Buddhism or Daoism. In this primitive usage, one could speculate that the term might have meant that there was more to existence than "met the eye." There was overarching order where chaos and disorder may have seemed to reign; there was thus justice where only brute power or chance ruled the scene; there was thus some ultimate purpose and structure to existence, despite how much the opposite seemed the truth of things.

In its early uses in English, "hierarchy" was linked to a systematic scheme by Christianized neo-Platonic philosophical theology of its day. It referred to a fixed order of theocratically ordained and progressive steps arrayed in terms of the lowest ranks of nature to the loftiest ranges of supernature. In both cases, the word entailed a metaphysical view of the world as vertical, one in which terms like "transcendence" were at home. Eventually, as one knows, it also came to be associated with the Roman Catholic order of ecclesiastical rank.

© Equinox Publishing Ltd. 2008, Unit 6, The Village, 101 Amies Street, London SW11 2JW

At the same time, and corresponding to this heavenly or metaphysical order, hierarchy often entailed a parallel—and sacred—political and social order. Because it modeled the sublime order of the divine nature, and was ordained by it, this order was considered fixed and eternal. Schemes of sacral kingship found in many parts of the world often reflect this hierarchic sensibility. Attempts at political or social change could easily be regarded as assaults on the divine plan. A deeply conservative vision of earthly life was therefore preordained by divine plan and sanctioned by the divine will.

But while Dumont's assertion of hierarchy may at first blush please some religious readers, others might be less eager to embrace Dumont's views.

> The idea of hierarchy, as the relation between the encompassing and encompassed, gives difficulty to many and even seems to outrage some. Why, in the first place—some would say—introduce such a confusing language? (Dumont 1971a, 67)

These would be people uncomfortable with any idea of an order that claimed legitimacy from sources outside the consensual, democratic determination of human beings, or with an order that fixed individuals into certain preordained levels absent their consent or even understanding, or that ranked one sort of person over another by virtue of some sort of unquestionable ascription, rather than their demonstrated achievements. Dumont's ideas about hierarchy may thus reek of a kind of medievalism reminiscent of our own pre-modern Western past. Historian Marc Bloch paints a picture of precisely this kind of world as it came to be in the European middle ages world of interrelated natural, social and theological domains, arrayed hierarchically and eternally unchanging (Bloch 1961). Certain kinds of egalitarians might, therefore, feel that Dumont's talk of a sacred *order* threatened democratic cultures; naturalists might suspect that Dumont's talk of a *sacred* order concealed a commitment to a reality beyond what human beings could know or challenge in some straightforwardly human way. To such genteel readers, or even to readers with conventional contemporary moral sensibilities, Dumont's theories might seem to present a particularly unwelcome set of ideas, indeed, perhaps singularly doomed to be "decidedly unpopular," as he well recognized. (Dumont 1979a, 806) Instead, Dumont believes that "the 'bet on hierarchy'" has "been a good one" (Dumont 1971a, 77).

Further, in his efforts to promote "hierarchy," or even merely to discuss it, rather than outright condemning it, is to grant it legitimacy, Dumont presents a real danger to things we hold dear. To give "hierarchy" a hearing, as Dumont would have us do, is to give an arguably odious moral notion a "platform"—as our modern-day guardians of public morality might say. It would violate our moral convictions and hard-won ethical sensibilities

© Equinox Publishing Ltd. 2008

seriously to entertain what Dumont seems to be saying about the value of adopting the viewpoint of hierarchy. As such, Dumont's ideas ought not be taken seriously or treated as neutral social fact that one might think about in the spirit of scientific detachment. Would we dignify cliterodectomy by treating it to the social scientific treatment Dumont affords hierarchy? Surely, our intellectual effort ought to be directed at *condemning* a horrid practice like female circumcision rather than thinking about it? If so for cliterodectomy, why not for Dumont's "hierarchy"?

Dumont's answer to such charges is disarmingly straightforward and unapologetic as one might expect from someone whose life has been devoted to classic anthropological method. As such the lack of any conspicuous taint of a political or ideological program recommends Dumont's classical appropriation of anthropological method for our consideration despite the reputation of, at least, the word, "hierarchy." This is not to say that no social, political or moral suggestions flow from Dumont's treatment of hierarchy. Indeed there are many, such as an affection for difference, diversity and life. But these overarching governing values of Dumont's world view do not dominate the subject matter of Dumont's theoretical discourses. They constitute, nonetheless, an ever-present horizon that draws him to give hierarchy a fair hearing. They are not a set of dictates forcing his analyses upon a Procrustean bed.

Consider his explanation of his orientation to hierarchy, despite the ill repute it—or at least a concept of "it"—enjoys in our world. First, as anthropologist, he takes an open attitude to others, and seeks to understand what their ways of living are trying to achieve: "Human institutions, whatever they are, have a meaning. The task of anthropologists, for some of us at any rate, is, so to speak, to construct the 'integral' of those meanings" (Delacampagne 1981, 5). That is to say, Dumont believes one ought to try to capture the "whole," the "totality"—the "integral"—of the meanings in human institutions before either praising or condemning them.

In this sense, second, we can look at societies as having opted for certain meanings over others—that different "types of society can be seen as [representing] so many different 'choices' among the potentialities of a common matrix..." (Delacampagne 1981, 5). In this sense, says Dumont "hierarchy does concern us, even if it is at the opposite pole of our choices" (Delacampagne 1981, 5). I would say perhaps *because* it is at that opposite tantalizing pole of ourselves. "Hierarchy" stands over against us, indicting us as our inverted mirror-image self, and thus fascinating us because it seems to be everything that we would not be, but what other folks have "decided" they would be. "How is it that 'they' could so differ from us?" we ask ourselves in a mixture of astonishment and perhaps a little horror, shared doubtless by those who first encountered the "other,"

© Equinox Publishing Ltd. 2008

like Fra Bartolomé de Las Casas, the famous, and some believe heroic, Spanish Dominican defender of the rights of Native Americans against the predations of Spanish colonialism in the New World. Tzvetan Todorov, despite his admiration for Las Casas, argued that he had a telling loss of nerve at a crucial point in his thinking about the "other." Motivated as he was to assert the humanity of the Native Americans, and thus their *equality* with the Spaniards, Las Casas could not really countenance the irreducible difference of the Native Americans. Instead, he minimized the differences between the Native Americans and the Spaniards to such an extent that he lost sight of the "other" as "other."

> there is an incontestable generosity on the part of Las Casas, who refuses to despise others simply because they are different. But he goes one step further and adds: moreover, they are not (or will not be) different. The postulate of equality involves the assertion of identity, and the second great figure of alterity, even if it is incontestably more attractive, leads to a knowledge of the other even less valid than the first. (Todorov 1999, 167)

No matter how good-hearted and generous Las Casas may have been, his seeing "them" as the same as "us" does "them" no favors at all.

Yet, third, Dumont does not stop with puzzlement or horror. He ventures forth beyond this to ask the question that puts ourselves and our own way of life at risk. Is it possible that societies based on hierarchy, such as classic India "might be showing us something we have chosen not to see, as it were, but something which *ex hypothesi* cannot be entirely absent with us... certainly blind spots" (Delacampagne 1981, 5). Is the disagreeable "other" simply *dis*agreeable because it represents something we have *agreed*, deliberately or not, to reject? Are we willing to subject our own comfortable arrangements to fundamental scrutiny, to examinations so radical that we might have to part with some of these cultural "comforts"? We may think, for example, that our individualism entails a broad rejection of all hierarchy. The individual is made subordinate to the group in holistic societies, but not in the our "freer" society of individuals [sic]. But, this belief proves to be delusional since what individualism in essence declares is just another kind of hierarchy—one in which sits the individual atop the group and subordinates it to itself. India's affirmation of hierarchy is scandalous in its open and explicit nature. But it can, thereby, force a partisan of individualism to recognize that individualism too requires hierarchical arrangements of things, however covertly this may be done. Individualists dare not admit what hierarchies they create. Yet, being exposed to Indian hierarchizing may force individualists to ask themselves whether they are quite free of the same operation?

Fourth, and finally, Dumont weighs the benefit of seeing that our ideology may not "tell us everything about reality." So, this realization "is a

© Equinox Publishing Ltd. 2008

way of seeing more clearly. Each type of society illuminates something of man..." (Delacampagne 1981, 5). Perhaps there are no perfect societies? Perhaps all social arrangements entail gains and losses—and such trade-offs, moreover, that cannot be mediated or synthesized. The philosopher and intellectual historian, Sir Isaiah Berlin, believed in a tragic social vision something like this—his "pluralism." We as humans live in a kind of "veil of tears," in a world in which there are many good values from which to choose. But, we are required to choose one, or at least a limited internally consistent set of such values, because some of the values we might choose mutually exclude one another. Berlin sees Machiavelli, for example, as presenting us with this sort of world: either one governs by a hard code of *Realpolitik*, or one governs as a Christian and turns the other cheek. As polar opposites, the two cannot be merged into one. Thus, if one tries only to govern by the Christian principles of compassion and love, Machiavelli believed that in a contest, a strong and unscrupulous "prince" would soon prevail. An "unarmed prophet," such as a Savonorola, may proclaim Christian spiritual rule, but will be undone by the first powerful "prince" who can force his own hard real political will upon events (Berlin 1979). In the same way, Dumont seems open to a kind of value pluralism described by Berlin. It is hard to imagine combining such radically opposed ideologies as holism with individualism. Instead, Dumont seems to counsel accepting the pain of imperfection, and perhaps to try to make the best of it! Let us then move on to engage more of the details of Dumont's mental universe.

"Hierarchy," a way of looking at things, rather than a "thing" itself

In at least two major articles, Dumont has made it clear that whatever else may be true about his writing about hierarchy, it at least embodies an ideology. It stands for a way of *imagining* social realities, for a way of *thinking* about social realities (Dumont 1971a, 1979a). That is to say, it is a way of *looking* at or *conceiving* the social, and thus religious, world, and thus a way human beings have chosen to arrange their lives by the rules of hierarchy. To the extent we blind ourselves to a hierarchical way certain real societies imagine and arrange themselves, we will simply not reflect what is "there." To the extent anti-hierarchical *ideology* intrudes upon our way of looking on other folks, we will not be equipped to see them as they, at least, either believe themselves to be or really are. We will venture forth without the epistemological gear that would make it possible to see hierarchy. As we will see in the next chapter, our Western *individualism* (and egalitarianism as well) is, for example, just one such ideology that creates an "impediment" to understanding societies constituted in very different—

© Equinox Publishing Ltd. 2008

Definitions of some key terms:

1. "Hierarchy" defined in a few words:

"Essentially, hierarchy is the encompassing of the contrary."

(Dumont 1979a, 809)

"Hierarchy" analyzed into its parts:

1. A system of difference, asymmetry (Dumont 1979a, 812), or inequality, understood as a system of oppositions (Dumont 1979a, 812) or contraries or levels (Dumont 1980, 244).

2. A system as basic as equality (Dumont 1980, 258).

3. A system that arises necessarily, (Dumont 1980, 244) whenever one makes a judgment of *value* (Dumont 1986).

4. A system in which, however, those differences are encompassed and subordinated to the whole. Hierarchy is synonymous to *holism* (Dumont 1979a, 806).

Example

The relation of right to left hand can be said to be "hierarchical" because although the two hands are *opposed* as "contraries," and considered "unequal" in "value" to each other, the right hand is culturally seen as superior to the left, the body needs both to attain wholeness, and thus the body constitutes the "whole" that "encompasses" both into the unity that is the human body.

2. The "Individual" and "Individualism," defined in a few words:

In the chapter entitled, "Of Individualism in Democratic Societies," in his *Democracy in America*, Alexis Tocqueville defined individualism in what is now a classic statement:

> Individualism is a novel expression, to which a novel idea has given birth. Our fathers were only acquainted with egotism. Egotism is a passionate and exaggerated love of self, which leads a man to connect everything with his own person, and to prefer himself to everything in the world. Individualism is a mature and calm feeling, which disposes each member of the community to sever himself from the mass of his fellow-creatures; and to draw apart with his family and his friends; so that, after he has thus formed a little circle of his own, he willingly leaves society at large to itself.... (Descombes 1999, 69; Dumont 1980, 17)

In Dumont's words, individualism is an ideology, a statement of our evaluation of human beings. Thus,

> every man is, in principle, an embodiment of humanity at large, and as such he is equal to every other man, and free." (Dumont 1977, 4)

© Equinox Publishing Ltd. 2008

> It declares that the concrete, empirical human individual is a supreme value for us in the West. As part of "our" Western ideology, it means that individualism—our view of the concrete human individual—is the product of our culture's long history. As part of our Western way of looking at the world, we have, over the centuries constructed what is for us a "dominant modern conception of man," as "the independent, autonomous and thus (essentially) nonsocial moral being... (Dumont 1986a, 62)

> **3. Individualism assumes hierarchy: an instructive paradox:**

> Although some people commonly misinterpret Dumont by opposing individualism and hierarchy, Dumont sees the situation of individualism in the West as an example of the very notion of hierarchy he develops most in India. That is to say, that individualism is *our* ideology, our supreme value is that we in the West hierarchize the individual *over* society. Granted *both* the individual and society are necessary for a *whole* human life, but in the West, Dumont is arguing, we have *ranked* the individual as *superior* to society. In India, and in its caste system, Dumont has argued that just the opposite ranking prevails: there, the society, group and so on are *ranked* over the individual. India's traditional social whole is the inverse of ours.

hierarchical—terms (Dumont 1970, 1979a, 806)

Thus, while it may be interesting to know how much Dumont favors a particular hierarchical way of looking at (and being in) the world (or not)—with all the political and moral implications such a stance might have—it would be best to begin trying to understand Dumont as at least advancing an epistemology. We should begin by seeing his effort, at least, as one of trying to *illuminate* an overlooked and often obscured way that people might shape their relations with one another. As Dumont says to his anthropological colleagues, "We are engaged in the discovery of a dimension of man that is fact obscured, scotomized among the moderns. This discovery is a long-term task for this very reason, and one which opens up a totality" (Dumont 1979a, 799). This means that some morally concerned critics of Dumont, such as Gerald Berreman or Rolland Lardinois, have started out on the wrong foot by implicating Dumont in proposing some specific form of concrete human living arrangements, understood as hierarchy (Berreman and Dumont 1962; Lardinois 1996). This may or may not be so. I have concluded that I simply have not been able to know whether this is true or not, with the possible exception of Dumont's longstanding opposition to totalitarianism. There, one may ask whether Dumont's interrogation of the egalitarian ideal is a sign of his own totalitarian instincts, or does it more likely occupy a standard position within French traditions of liberal criticism of the kind of Stalinist Marxism typical of France, not to

© Equinox Publishing Ltd. 2008

mention his frequent and darkly repeated warnings about the tendencies that produced Nazi Germany (Dumont 1979a, 802)? Is Dumont therefore to be aligned with someone like Raymond Aron, his equally contrary but impeccably liberal, contemporary and associate? Is Dumont perhaps better lined up with more contemporary liberal thinkers like Tzvetan Todorov, Luc Ferry, and Bernard-Henri Lévy, all of whom regard Dumont highly? Not only has Dumont associated himself with Aron's admiration for German thinkers like Max Weber, but he has also written for the French liberal periodical, *Commentaire*. Likewise, Dumont has also staked out a position over against the worship of power, common to Todorov, Ferry and Lévy in the anti-Nietzschean camp of modern-day French philosophers. The modern-day French liberalism which these thinkers represent is little known in the United States. Part of the burden of this discussion of Dumont as moralist is to bring to light the traditions of today's evolving French liberalism. (Ferry and Renaut 1990, 1997; Todorov 2002)

About hierarchy, Dumont has always said that he thinks it takes the side of life. It permits movement and differential relationships, with subtle changes in priority between people, the (give-and-take) about which Americans speak. For Dumont, this means he is committed to tolerance, for a radical acceptance of difference. It is perhaps for this reason that he can take the Indian hierarchy more seriously than others, since whatever else may be true of it, Indian hierarchy as embodied in caste is inclusive: "All groups have their place however inferior"(Parkin 2003, 118). As Robert Parkin, one of Dumont's most capable critics points out, in India it is generally not the lower castes who seek to cut the ties that bind them to the system. It is rather the upper castes who seek to "ditch" their obligations to the lower castes in an effort to individuate themselves from the system. It is those who supposedly sit atop the system and benefit most by it who are the *least* tolerant, and would just as soon hive off on their own. When all players abide by the rules of the system, however, what dominates is a sense of all-inclusiveness—of tolerance, rather than elimination (Parkin 2003, 88f).

What kills relationships, in his mind, is the selfish individualism that often comes with insistence upon equality at every moment. There is no give, no view of the long run, no opening to the future, rather, a constant niggling keeping of score, to keep even, so to speak. Instead, hierarchy taught Dumont that relationships need to be seen through time, through a long process of giving and receiving—and giving again—in which debts may never finally be equalized or balanced out. In this way the circulation of social life blood never ceases, because give-and-take never cease. Of course, there are times when this necessary give-and-take becomes so unbalanced that social intercourse halts: branding certain people as "tak-

© Equinox Publishing Ltd. 2008

ers" or feeling that one is empty because one "loves too much" are familiar enough symptoms of this gross imbalance in social give-and-take. But short of gross imbalances, continuing in a relationship from Dumont's perspective means that one trusts that equality would be the statistical result of a long process, at the endpoint, so to speak. Beyond these speculations about the possible political implications of Dumont's thinking, as well as his own political affiliations, what is certain is that Dumont is putting forth an epistemology—a way of seeing how we shape and understand social life.

Transgression and the uses of taboo

Given these critiques, how, and why, we might ask, are Dumont and his "attempts to sell hierarchy" to students of culture worthy of serious study? Should not an apparently retrograde, transgressive and morally offensive notion like hierarchy, be dismissed from attempts better to *understand*, much less promote it? That is the matter to which I should like to turn now.

Dumont is fully aware of the ill-repute into which—the word, at least— "hierarchy" has fallen, even if he is unwilling to pull back from his program:

> It is appropriate to keep in mind our aversion to hierarchy. Not only does this aversion explain our difficulty in deepening our understanding of hierarchy but we are facing a kind of taboo, an unmistakable censure, and caution requires the adoption of a circumspect approach, the avoidance of any provocative statements or premature judgments. (Dumont 1980, 239)

In another place, Dumont casts a different light on the resistance his treatment of hierarchy in *Homo Hierarchicus*—"*H.H.*"—inspires by hypothesizing a scenario worthy of his being a somewhat remote offspring of the Collège de Sociologie.

> In general, the case might be put against me by saying that what *H.H.* proposed was far too removed from what certain readers were prepared to accept, that the book has, so to speak, put itself beyond the range of implicit consensus, with the result that many readers are ill-prepared to understand or follow it.(Dumont 1971a, 64–65)

Like the cultural *avant-garde* with whom he kept casual company in the 1930s, Dumont would not be surprised that his work might seem unconventional. Indeed, part of what I am arguing is that Dumont's being *unconventional* in the spirit of the Collège de Sociologie is, in part, the whole point of his radical treatment of hierarchy.

Such passages should then alert readers to recall Dumont's youth in the Paris of the early 1930s. I have urged that Dumont was less influenced by the occultist, René Guénon, than by his own teacher, Durkheim's often rambunctious nephew, Marcel Mauss. Among others, Jim Clifford has

© Equinox Publishing Ltd. 2008

established connections between Mauss and the Parisian *avant-garde* of the early twentieth century in his classic essay, "On Ethnographic Surrealism" (Clifford 1988). Clifford and others have shown how other students of Mauss made up a radical wing of the second generation of the Durkheimian "team." These were Dumont's age-mates and acquaintances, Roger Caillois and Georges Bataille, co-founders of the Collège de Sociologie. In those days Roger Caillois, but most of all, Georges Bataille, celebrated the social and cultural utility of *transgression*. As self-styled rebels, close to artistic movements such as surrealism and Dada, they sought to revive Western cultural life by challenging it with notions and practices that were flatly *transgressive*—that offended conventional thinking and action.

It requires little imagination to see Dumont following the lead of Roger Caillois and Georges Bataille years later and thrusting a "transgressive" notion of hierarchy upon the bourgeois academy. Rolland Lardinois also thinks that Dumont may have taken up with hierarchy because of René Guénon's similar affection for the notion (Lardinois 1996, 29). In the same way as these radical Durkheimians and others in the agitated milieu of the 1930s sought to stir up creative thought and action in the France of their day, so also does Dumont arguably seek to stun his colleagues into new lines of thinking about social life by trying to "sell" the academic community on his transgressive notion of hierarchy. Dumont has always been keenly aware that his research program inevitably faced "a kind of taboo" within our own society, and thus risked facing "an unmistakable censure," as it indeed has at the hands of the critics we have just reviewed. But, this did not deter him, any more than it would have deterred the likes of Caillois and Bataille. Yet, these days, Dumont acts prudently. He was not about to advocate the equivalent of Bataille's plan for human sacrifice in the Place de la Concorde! No longer the brash youth, Dumont urged "circumspection" in pressing his case for hierarchy. There would be no "provocation," as he tells us. Years after his first introduction of the idea of hierarchy, Dumont reflects on his tactics following upon the controversy its promotion has caused: "I chose to move forward slowly and let the brief grow heavier, the ground settle and the horizon grow more distinct" (Dumont 1980, 239). All well and good. Nonetheless, such calculations should not lead us to overlook the obvious connections between Dumont and the program of cultural transgression at the heart of the efforts of the Collège de Sociologie. All this then only raises more acutely problems of dealing with the subject of this chapter, hierarchy. Granted that it may be a notion of ill-repute, taboo and transgression, how and why then do we study it at all?

© Equinox Publishing Ltd. 2008

"Tout comprendre, c'est tout pardoner"

It is plausible that one might argue that popularly repellant notions like hierarchy ought not be studied by means of empathy. Would empathizing with these morally noxious objects not risk courting, if not constituting, agreement with them? Would not "empathy" lead us down a slippery slope to "sympathy." The French have a saying, "tout comprendre, c'est tout pardoner"—"to understand everything is to pardon everything." Are Dumont's attempts to "understand" hierarchy, caste and perhaps even other unsavory notions, really stealthy attempts to applaud them—to "pardon" them? That, at any rate, seems behind part of the resistance to Dumont's work on hierarchy—he does not slavishly condemn these notions and institutions, nor does he beat his breast in repentance for trying to understand them *before* he might go on to evaluate them.

Part of the burden of this chapter is to open up this kind of question to consideration. It is hard to see how Dumont's thought could be useful to the study of religion if the critics of the moral status of his major concepts and approach to the study of society were as flawed as some believe. If, on the other hand, despite these charges, Dumont escapes morally untainted, then our conventional thinking about hierarchy would have to be re-examined. This chapter urges precisely a re-examination of the notion of hierarchy as Dumont understands it.

Everybody thinks they know what "hierarchy" is. But, do they?

Given the way "hierarchy" offends the egalitarian ear of liberal Western readers, one would not expect enthusiastic rallying to the idea. Hierarchy transgresses everything most progressive folk in the West hold dear. Witness to this, shortly after the appearance of his classic work on the Indian caste system, *Homo Hierarchicus,* some left-wing American critics accused Dumont of seeking to defend the ethical "evils" of the inequality inherent in the essentially hierarchical Hindu "caste system." Recall alone the murmurings in Parisian academic circles about Dumont's youthful flirtations with occultist René Guénon casts doubts on the scientific status of Dumont's efforts by insinuating that key features of Dumont's thought originated in the mystical orientalist musings of the profoundly anti-modern Guénon (Lardinois 1996).

Aside from the general question of the proper academic attitude towards offensive notions like hierarchy, there is the looming question about it—namely, what is this "*it*"? Upon hearing or first reading that Dumont wishes to explore "hierarchy," few think that there is something to be learned about this notion: "everybody *knows* what hierarchy is" [sic]. A survey of

© Equinox Publishing Ltd. 2008

Dumont's first critics reveals that only one of them—anthropologist Pauline Kolenda—even bothered to try to tease out what Dumont might have meant by the term. Kolenda herself might have been extreme in her sifting through of all the *seven* meanings of "hierarchy" in Dumont's work, since she devoted an entire critique of Dumont's classic on hierarchy, *Homo Hierarchicus*, to elaborating them (Kolenda 1976)! Nonetheless, the singularity of Kolenda's effort to try to understand what Dumont might have been saying, rather than presuming the commonplace meaning of the term, "hierarchy," tells this writer a great deal about how Dumont has been read by most of his critics.

For this reason, I am urging readers not to get side-tracked by the commonplace sense of the term, "hierarchy" itself, and its everyday meanings—at least not at the very beginning of their reading experience of Dumont. His choice of terminology, for example, might be inadvertent (or perhaps not). Whatever the case, this decision may have distracted readers from what Dumont wants to say because it is so easy for us to get fixated on the term itself as usually understood. If readers do get side-tracked in this way, the fault, of course, lies substantially with Dumont. He is, as I have argued, at least partly a product of the radical Durkheimian traditions of the Collège de Sociologie and its deliberate deployment of transgressions, whether of ritual, institutional or even linguistic sorts. Here, the term, "hierarchy," induces the same discomfiting effect. True, despite his protests, some of what Dumont wants to say may well be caught in the ordinary usage of the term, "hierarchy." Indeed, perhaps *all* of it is? But, is it? This is part of the business of this part of the present chapter.

So, presuming for the moment that Dumont's idea of hierarchy differs substantially from the everyday, it is worth seeing this offense as intentional. It may not have been *wise* or prudent for Dumont to have chosen such an obviously offensive and controversial word to name the relationship he seeks to elaborate—even given the vicissitudes of translation from French. But, if I am right about linking Dumont to the Collège de Sociologie, epitomized by one of its major "bad boy" transgressors, like the pornographer Georges Bataille, no one connected with this group in the early 1930s was easily given to prudence. Batallie's ambition to re-establish a lost sense of the sacred by instituting human sacrifice in a major Parisian traffic "circle," for instance, exemplifies the least prudent of all the efforts of the Collège de Sociologie. So, while staying loyal to Dumont's terminology, my purpose will be to try to stay focused on the concept and *relationship* that Dumont wants to explicate, despite whatever transgressive intentions Dumont may also have had in mind for the usage he has selected.

Here, then, I want to interrogate Dumont's idea of hierarchy, asking not

© Equinox Publishing Ltd. 2008

only what he means by the term, but whether his critics on the left have been justified in their moral condemnation of the notion as expounded by Dumont. Are not such notions as hierarchy or such institutions as caste so egregious that they must be straightforwardly condemned rather than studied? Does something sinister lurk behind Dumont's putatively scientific writing about hierarchy? Before we can engage these problems, we will need to ask what Dumont's concept of hierarchy is, beginning first with what *he* says it is.

Hierarchy: What it ain't, what it is

Dumont knows that the term "hierarchy" will draw fire. It is, after all, a form of inequality expressed in the context of a society for which all manner of equality is the social norm, in theory if not in practice. In such societies as ours where the egalitarian principle forms the norm of so many institutions, practices and beliefs, most forms of inequality will tend to look the same (Dumont 1980, 251). Dumont realizes this, and so tries to allay the understandable fears and suspicions arising from this fact by addressing standard misconceptions about what he wants the term to mean. He thus begins by exploring the question of the meaning of the term in a negative way—what hierarchy is not. Thus, Dumont's conception of hierarchy is not the same as "hierarchy" used in these familiar senses: (1) rank or social stratification, (2) a relationship typified by power over another, (3) a chain of beings of gradually descending dignity.

First, Dumont's notion of hierarchy is simply *not* the same as one that circulates in the world of ordinary talk or even in sociology—the name of a scheme of ranking or social stratification.

> I believe that hierarchy is not, essentially, a chain of superimposed commands, nor even a chain of beings of decreasing dignity, nor yet a taxonomic tree, but a relation that can succinctly be called "the encompassing of the contrary." (Dumont 1980, 239)

Hierarchy in Dumont's sense may not entail *any* command structure at all. It is not a matter of ordering people about. Thus, when Dumont speaks of a hierarchical relation between right and left hand— with the right hand being considered superior to the left—there is no question of rank or command structure between the two hands.

Second, hierarchy does not necessarily entail a relationship of power of one over another. In Dumont's view of things, right and left hands exist in a relationship of hierarchy. Right and left are unequal, and a kind of higher value is afforded the right over the left. But just as in the case of hierarchy not involving a command structure of the right over the left hand, so also is their relationship not conditioned by a differential of *power*. While the right hand may be, for example, universally considered superior to the left, it

© Equinox Publishing Ltd. 2008

has no intrinsic or necessary power over the left hand.

Third, even less is hierarchy a "chain of beings of decreasing dignity" (Dumont 1980, 239). Dumont is not thinking about the great chain of being of the neo-platonic and Christian medieval world, where all beings are arrayed in a graduated scale of reality from the lowest form of creation to the highest levels of divinity. The appearance of neo-medievalism in Dumont's thought is just that—a superficial similarity, based largely on a coincidence of terminology. There is little or nothing in Dumont's writing to suspect him of crypto-Catholicism or of neo-clericalism. Resorting again to the example of the right and left hands, for example, we all know that the right hand may enjoy a kind of favoritism, the left hand has its own dignity too. In folk classification, the right hand is the commonly preferred hand, such as in locutions like "my right hand man." But likewise in the world of folk classification, to be left-handed carries its own mysterious power as the exceptional hand, and so on. Such differentials turn up in the oddest places, such as in baseball, where right-handed pitchers are "normal," since the predominant number of pitchers are right-handed. Yet, despite the "normality" right-handed pitchers, left-handers are attributed with a kind of "magic" in the form of being considered possessors of all sorts of unusual craft and guile that make them unusually successful at deceiving batters. Left-handers likewise often have unusually contorted windups, or are considered "flakey," or bear the name corresponding to their delivery, e.g. Lefty Grove, Lefty O'Doul and so on. No one has ever been called "Righty" So and So.

Fourth, and finally, hierarchy is not some sort of "taxonomic tree" (Dumont 1980, 239). It is not a purely formal array of objects or relationships, such as genus/species and such. As we will see, Dumont's "hierarchy" concerns matters of substantive relationship of value. For Dumont, the right and left hands are not principally important with respect to one another for the sake of the *formal* nature of that relationship, e.g. opposition, but both because of their *formally* being opposed to one another, and their possessing *qualitative* differences between themselves and in their relationship to the whole body of which they are a part (Dumont 1980, 244). As Dumont will explain, right and left hands are not *equally* balanced off against each other, and to which they are both subordinated. Greater value is generally assigned to the right over the left. We pledge allegiance, shake hands, sign ourselves with the right hand, but the left hand is the hand of "defilement." But we do not function as "whole" humans unless have both hands.

Because Dumont's idea of hierarchy is really so distant from ordinary senses of the term, I would urge readers to hold back on condemning Dumont's idea of hierarchy. If what I have laid out about the opposition

© Equinox Publishing Ltd. 2008

between right and left hands is part of what Dumont means by "hierarchy," there is then not *one* idea of "hierarchy," but perhaps many. Some of these notions of hierarchy may be worthy of moral condemnation, but since there are many, some may not. Dumont believes his is one of those notions of hierarchy that escapes the standard moral condemnation reserved for hierarchies as reprobate systems of domination. Thus, some number of those other notions of hierarchy may not deserve the disdain often dealt out to "hierarchy" as commonly understood. Still, if this be so, one wonders why Dumont chose to use such a charged and controversial term? Perhaps, this is yet again another part of the legacy of the transgressive style he learnt from the Collège de Sociologie? By this logic, Dumont does not mind giving offense to "bourgeois" sensibilities. Too bad for the bourgeoisie! But that would be the matter of further speculation that we might prudently put aside for the while. The question to which we are now directed after surveying what senses of "hierarchy" Dumont rejects is what he then means by "hierarchy"?

Hierarchy in general

Let me begin with a definition Dumont himself has given, and then analyze it into what I take to be its salient parts.

> What I call hierarchical opposition is the opposition between a set (and more particularly a whole) and an element of this set (or of this whole); the element is not necessarily simple, it can be a subset. This opposition is logically analyzable into contradictory partial aspects: on the one hand, the element is identical to the set in that it forms part thereof (any vertebrate is an animal), on the other hand, there is difference, or strictly, contrariety (a vertebrate is not *solely* an animal, an animal is not *necessarily* a vertebrate). This double relation—identity and contrariety—it is stricter when a proper whole is concerned than when a more or less arbitrary set is involved.... This double relation is a logical scandal, which is both an explanation for the disfavor it finds, and the reason for the interest it deserves: every relation between an element and the set of which it is a part introduces hierarchy and is logically inadmissible. Essentially, hierarchy is the *encompassing of the contrary*. (Dumont 1979a, 809)

Out of this long citation, and from other places, the following points can be broken out about what Dumont's idea of 'hierarchy' is

1. A system of difference, asymmetry (Dumont 1979a, 812), or inequality, understood as a system of oppositions (Dumont 1979a, 812) or contraries or levels (Dumont 1980, 244);

2. A system as basic as equality (Dumont 1980, 258);

3. A system that arises necessarily, (Dumont 1980, 244) whenever one makes a judgment of *value* (Dumont 1986);

© Equinox Publishing Ltd. 2008

4. A system in which, however, those differences are encompassed and sub-ordinated to the whole. Hierarchy is synonymous to *holism* (Dumont 1979a, 806);

5. A system not built up from transactions, but transactions are governed by the fact of hierarchic relations of exchangers (Dumont 1971a, 65).

"Vive la différence!": Hierarchies as schemes of difference and inequality

Before anything else, Dumont's idea of "hierarchy" is a system of *inequality*. It is a scheme in which, as he says, "egalitarianism is not in place"(Dumont 1979a, 806). Dumont makes no excuses for saying that he is interested in social systems governed and/or constituted by difference, asymmetry or inequality. Rather than beating his breast for bringing inequality into polite conversation, Dumont declares that he wants to understand such systems. To him, systems of inequality are many. At the very least, they are systems of difference. They may be asymmetrical, such as in male/female relationships in traditional societies. Or, in modern political arrangements, we might mention the federal/local (state, provincial or cantonal) relationship. Or, further, we may speak of "levels" in a relationship, such as in degrees of intimacy, or where members of the relationship are opposed to each other, such as contraries of various sorts like priest and king, for example. All these relationships are at least potentially "hierarchic" in Dumont's sense, since they are relations of difference or inequality. Appreciation of difference is thus where Dumont's conception of hierarchy can be said to take its start. Outside of his great work on the Indian caste system, *Homo Hierarchicus*, in choosing examples of the inequality of hierarchy, Dumont selects disarmingly uncontroversial examples of the inequality that typifies his sense of "hierarchy." Among these are the relation between right and left hands, the relation between asymmetric wholes and parts of the whole.

Here is how Dumont approaches at least one prime example of what he means by "hierarchy"—the relation of right and left hands. One might, for example, be tempted to see the right and left hands of the human body as equal. They fall into place with the rest of the natural symmetry of our form—two eyes, two feet, two wrists, two ankles, two knees, two elbows, two arms, two legs, two breasts, and so on, all neatly balanced off against one another, equals in casting our "fateful symmetry." Each is in principle no better than the other; each is really only a second version of the first; each perfectly matched with the other; each is virtually the same, and thus not really different, from the other.

Yet, from a cultural viewpoint, unlike almost every one of these bodily pairs, the right and left hands are virtually and universally seen as differ-

© Equinox Publishing Ltd. 2008

ent from and unequal to each other, and in many cases radically opposed to each other. In turn, this bodily opposition generates a symbolism of left and right that finds broad cross-cultural resonance. Cultures generally *value* the right over the left, as "normal." Where, elsewhere, sameness, balance and symmetry and equality reign, with right and left hand asymmetry, imbalance, difference, opposition, and most importantly, *inequality* in *value* dominate the discourse human cultures have brought to bear on the two hands of the human body. The expression, "my right hand man" signals a value preference over someone who might be called one's "left hand man"—oddly enough an expression without any currency at all. In speaking symbolically of the left hand as the "hand of defilement" we are likewise *evaluating* it as a hand with certain kinds of necessary, yet unpleasant functions. In *choosing* to make a sign of friendship that of shaking hands with the right, rather than the left, societies place special value on the right. Imagine rejecting the right hand shake and offering the left instead. In some places this would signal disdain rather than friendship. At any rate, all these reflect cultural biases—*valuations*—against the left hand and in favor of the right. This is part of what Dumont wants us to grasp as essential to his notion of "hierarchy"—unequal valuation.

This differential, unequal value of right and left once more points up the *normal* cultural nature of hierarchy. From every abstract consideration that one might imagine, right and left hands should be *equals*, yet human cultures have other ideas about this relationship. That other idea is *hierarchy*, not equality. It is difference, not sameness, contrariety, not parallelism and so on. Human cultures the world over thus assert their comfort with hierarchy by asserting their need to enshrine difference, for differential valuation—and this does not seem pathological, at least if we are to begin by judging from an example like that of the right and left hands. The upshot of this suggests that for some reason or another we perhaps will never fully understand, human beings require, in some measure, a sense of differential value in their conception of the right order of things. Human cultures, Dumont would say, need hierarchy. This assertion of inequality is not accidental, but something that emerges necessarily in cultures the world over (Dumont 1980, 248).

Hierarchy as system in which difference and inequality are encompassed

Demonstrating how difference makes sense is the easy part of laying out what Dumont means by "hierarchy." After all, there are many examples of what one might call, and Dumont does, "distinctive opposition"(Dumont 1971a, 77; 1979a, 806). But for Dumont, "hierarchy" is not to be reduced to this kind of opposition. "Distinctive oppositions" would include inde-

© Equinox Publishing Ltd. 2008

pendently opposed pairs of items that might, for example, be arrayed in matched columns to make up symbolic systems. For example, such oppositions might be various sorts of "'binary classifications'... more or less homologous to one another" (Dumont 1979a, 808). Here one recalls the abstract binary oppositions so important for structuralists like Lévi-Strauss: pure/impure, high/low, born of the earth/born of woman, black/white and so on (Dumont 1971a, 77). The opposition of right/left might also serve here, but understood such that right and left are internally *independent* of one another and/or of any whole of which they might happen to be a part.

But, Dumont does not mean to identify this sort of "distinctive opposition" with the way opposition is handled in his notion of "hierarchy." For Dumont, "hierarchy" is not just a scheme of difference, nor even less is it abstract. For him, "hierarchy" necessarily involves relating the items of difference to one another with respect to a larger whole in which they inhere. In his own words, Dumont says that "in 'hierarchy' something that can be called analytically a contradiction (or a complementarity) is encompassed within a unity of a higher order" (Dumont 1971a, 78). Dumont insists upon relationship between differential elements. But, what kind of relationship does Dumont have in mind?

This relation of contrary or opposed items, subjected all the while to a whole, is what Dumont means by "hierarchy" as "the *encompassing of the contrary*" (Dumont 1979a, 809). It is thus *encompassment* that brings differences into a relation with respect to a larger whole, but in a differential, unequal, asymmetrical way. So, the problem before us is to comprehend what Dumont means by defining hierarchy as involving an encompassing—and an encompassing of the contrary at that (Dumont 1979a, 806; 1980, 239)! In stressing that "encompassment" is essential to hierarchy, Dumont, therefore, shows us that he is perhaps less concerned with difference and inequality, than with the promise of harmony and conciliation. He is interested in social systems that are not dominated by the conflict model, but by the model of tolerance, co-operation and harmony. Thus, to repeat Dumont's definition of what he means by the kind of opposition typical of his idea of "hierarchy": First, in Dumont's words, he says that "What I call hierarchical opposition is the opposition between a set (and more particularly a whole) and an element of this set (or of this whole)...". Thus, the poles opposed are seen *in relation to* greater entities—here parts to wholes. Second, " This opposition is logically analyzable into contradictory partial aspects" (Dumont 1980, 239). Dumont uses the example of the "vertebrate"/"animal" difference, indeed "strictly, contrariety," since "a vertebrate is not *solely* an animal, an animal is not *necessarily* a vertebrate." We may use the example of right and left hands, where either can be said to be part of a larger whole—the body—although they are not "solely" so.

© Equinox Publishing Ltd. 2008

And, beyond being strictly opposed to one another, in Dumont's way, they are opposed to the body itself. The right hand is part of the body, but a human body is still human—although not perfect or ideal—if one or the other hand is lacking. Third, Dumont concludes from this that "essentially, hierarchy is the *encompassing of the contrary*" (Dumont 1979a, 809). That is to say that no matter how different right and left hands may be, and no matter how they relate to the body as a whole, Dumont wants to characterize their relationship as "hierarchical." This is to say that in concrete cultural situations, both right and left hands are opposed and differ, but are not equal or symmetrical to one another. The right hand enjoys a kind of "preeminence" that is culturally "necessary." Yet, the body as a whole remains the reference point for the relation of the hands, since it and its needs "encompass" any particular needs of its two hands. Moreover, the right hand is ranked above the left, and in being so "is more representative" of the whole (Dumont 1979a, 810).

One curious upshot of Dumont's view is that since the contraries so encompassed are not symmetrical, their reversal produces interesting results. If right and left hands were a symmetrical relation, nothing much would result in their reversal. But, we know this is not the case when, for instance, left hand is said to be preeminent over the right. There, as in the case of baseball pitchers mentioned earlier, the preeminence of the left portends strange consequences, such as all the "superstitions" attending left handed pitchers as being "crafty" or unorthodox in their deliveries. Something of the same applies, in social settings such as the "lord of misrule" or "king for a day," where social roles are reversed, but where the behavior is hardly symmetrical. Those enjoying the reversal of roles do not simply introduce a variant of the previous order, but in many cases destroy order altogether by producing chaos.

Another example, here closer to the domain of religion, would be that between pure and impure, say, for example, in Hinduism. Again, although pure and impure *look* like "distinctive oppositions," like a symmetrical pair of contraries, they are not. The pure is *normally* considered superior to the impure, and is thus the marked or preferred category; as embodiment of purity, the Brāhmin is exalted, and his virtue comes to identify the norms of the Hindu totality. The brahmin thus not only stands for the pure, but the whole as well in that he encompasses both contraries of pure and impure. The impure is looked on as a residuum or as a mere negation or threat to the purity of the brahmin. The pure and impure are themselves, therefore, parts of the larger whole called something like Hinduism. There is no pollution—*im*purity—if there is no purity; there is no need of purification rites, unless there is the impurity of pollution to eliminate.

Given Dumont's socio-logic of hierarchy, reversal should produce its

© Equinox Publishing Ltd. 2008

own remarkable effects, as indeed it does, for instance, in India. In the domain of the lower, impure castes, the higher, pure, caste members are subordinated to their inferiors, much as the right hand is subordinated to the left in the domain of say, so-called, black magic. A spectacular example is afforded us in the feast that celebrates Lord Krishna's divine playfulness and prankishness—Holī. Here, the roles of higher and lower castes are reversed in a riotous ritual of status inversion, reminiscent of the European festivals of the lord of misrule. Over a period of 24 hours or so of creative ritual chaos and unbridled disorder, "encompassed" wives beat their "encompassing" husbands, "pure" Brāhmins get polluted with excreta by their "impure" lower caste clients; children berate their elders; young women pursue their terrified male counterparts. In Holī's riotous day of inverted hierarchies, what had been impure and inferior—lower castes, women, the young—was now elevated over those that were normally pure and superior—the Brāhmins, men, the village elders—analogously to the way some left-handed pitchers are attributed with superior powers by simple virtue of their left-handedness. In Holī, other reversals rule as well: "purification" is achieved by polluting, such as by "washing" high caste individuals in human filth and other abominable substances. Significantly, however, none of this attack on the "whole"—the traditional hierarchy of village Hindu society—results in the destruction of that "whole." If anything, the unity of the "whole" is reaffirmed and strengthened; traditional hierarchy is re-established with perhaps even greater affirmation (Marriott 1966). What should then be noted is how the opposition posited by Dumont as essential to hierarchical opposition is not the simple "distinctive opposition" of binary symmetry, but instead an unbalanced system of difference in which superior and inferior interact in ways that reflect their participation in another sort of social relationship than most social theorists of our time have had the occasion—or esthetic distance from their own Western perspectives—to recognize.

Part of the burden of what I am arguing, both implicitly and explicitly, then is that Dumont's vision ought to be taken seriously, and not written off as a kind of neo-medievalism or nostaligic conservatism. It remains to be seen whether it may or may not have fatal difficulties. But, in part, because Dumont is not the clearest of writers, I am trying to make as much sense as I can of his proposals about hierarchy and here, in particular, the idea of hierarchy as encompassment of the contrary. I am encouraged about the value of this project in part by the unhappiness that sometimes seems to hang over our politics so typically conditioned by in the conflict model of social life. This is why the occasional glimmers of other ways of going about political life that shine forth from time to time catch one's attention. In this vein, something of the spirit of Dumont's vision here was recent-

© Equinox Publishing Ltd. 2008

ly and unwittingly grasped by an OpEd piece in the *Los Angeles Times* by social psychologist, Jonathan Haidt discussing the state of American politics: "As Democrats change the drapes on Capitol Hill and relegate to Republicans to minority status, both parties would do well to look to the ancient East for advice on how opposites should—and should not—work together" (Haidt 2007, M3). So, with Dumont's admittedly eccentric position fully in view in his notion of hierarchy involving "encompassment," let me try to lay out what I think it means, so that readers may begin their own process of evaluation of it.

"Hierarchy" and value

Two further points—on value and on holism. While the notion of "encompassment" may seem obscure, Dumont tries to make it less so by linking both it and hierarchy with the notion of value or evaluation. Dumont believes that although modern folk may decry hierarchy, they actually still use it, but without fully recognizing it. Life often presents us with hard choices. In life, we make critical and consequential value judgments because we opt for one good over another. Here we may reprise the earlier example of Isaiah Berlin's "pluralist" dilemma. One such classic quandary for modern Western societies has been that between the relative value of liberty to equality. Typically, the story goes that my choice of liberty, for example, means that I cannot—at least at the same time and in the same place—value equality with the same force. The same is, of course, true, vice versa. The two values cannot be maximized at the same time in the same place. One must yield. To be free is at the same time to be free to excel; to excel often means to distinguish oneself from others—to be *un*equal to others. To value freedom means to subordinate it to equality. Choosing means both that we embrace what we value, but also that, to some extent, we let go of what we do not. Were I to choose to maximize equality, I would necessarily be subordinating it to liberty. In making value judgments, there is then gain, but loss too. The loss may not be permanent, but it is loss nonetheless.

I believe Dumont would be tempted to add both a *caveat* and a further observation. First, to the *caveat*. Typically, in the West, the choice between values, such as those between liberty and equality entails the *elimination* or suppression of the value not chosen. Thus, for extreme liberal right-wing economists, the elevation of liberty as a paramount value entails *no* attention to the needs for equality. In its purest form, the so-called "free market" is precisely a structure in which economic liberty rules *absolutely*, and considerations of equality are purged from consideration. All ameliorating social legislation or regulation of the market are to be eschewed. On the other hand, in a pure, classic communist economic

© Equinox Publishing Ltd. 2008

world, economic life is to be governed *absolutely* by the value of equality. At any point where economic liberty might threaten human equality, that liberty must be curtailed or simply eliminated. Thus, whether one represents the economic right or left, in the West, the tendency—at least on the extremes—has been to crush, eliminate or suppress the opposition. Thus, while Dumont would see such choices as potentially expressing a hierarchy in his sense—"the encompassing of the contrary"(Dumont 1979a, 809)—they seek to destroy the possibility of hierarchy by eliminating the encompassed value, whatever that may be.

At this point, if he were trying to persuade readers of the virtues of hierarchy, Dumont might make the following comment on the back of this *caveat*. He might be tempted to observe, first of all, that the common absolutism of the left and right results from a denial of *hierarchy*—from the refusal to "encompass" or include the other. Instead, what the West, in these cases, does is *purge* or eliminate our others. But, this denial of hierarchy, Dumont would add, has been demonstrably responsible for enormous pain and suffering in our modern societies—with dubious claims of significant overall improvement in the lives of us all. For Dumont, this is not desirable. Conflict, in itself, is no virtue. If our economic and political extremists would let the historical experience of India speak to them, they would see that—in the long run—there is more to be gained by accepting a Hindu hierarchical way of dealing with opposition, difference, otherness and the like. Better to tolerate, include, encompass than to try to crush, eliminate, liquidate and so on. Better the compromises of "federal" solutions to communal differences within the nation-state than to a leveling nationalism that seeks to dissolve communal differences into the national "whole." Thus, better Canada, Switzerland or the United States than France!

Thus, Dumont's notion of hierarchy is important to the extent that it recognizes and openly confronts the fact that societies arrange themselves by opting for one choice over another, and by "the encompassing of the contrary" (Dumont 1979a, 809). By this I do not primarily mean the way that societies *represent* their social arrangements—however it would be desirable that they acknowledged Dumont's hierarchy explicitly—but how these arrangements really are. For every time that we *evaluate* something, every time we value one thing over another, we are assigning *unequal* values to them. And, thus every time we *evaluate*, we are thinking hierarchically—unless we take the eliminationist route. Evaluating the right hand over the left, as we have seen, is just such one example of what Dumont is getting at here. Dumont is thus trying to break through the resistance we, as egalitarians, may throw up for admitting that we are acting contrarily to our own stated values. Ironically, another way of bringing this point home

© Equinox Publishing Ltd. 2008

is to call attention to the fact that when we egalitarians assert the value of equality, we are *ipso facto* hierarchizing it *above* the value of hierarchy! In choosing egalitarian values, we are *ipso facto* deciding to put the values of hierarchy to one side. The problem with being egalitarians is that it is awkward to admit that even the assertion of equality as a value involves us in hierarchical thinking, which, if Dumont is right, it does.

Now, Dumont takes a further step and says that every time we evaluate things differently, we not only are hierarchizing things, but that we *ipso facto* generate *encompassment*. Thus when classical political theorists write of "goods" and "services," yet value "goods" *over* "services," they may be both, *ipso facto,* thinking hierarchically about good and services, and *encompassing* "services" by "goods" "at the same time." When Adam Smith says that "work encompasses exchange" or when Marx says that "production encompasses production," they are saying, respectively, in Smith's case, that work is to be valued more than exchange and, in Marx's case, that production is to be valued more than consumption. For both Smith and Marx, respectively, a hierarchy seems to be established. This is why Dumont can make the, at first, mysterious-seeming claim that "Every time a notion gains importance it acquires the capacity to encompass its contrary" (Dumont 1980, 245). This means that while both right and left hands seem like mere "facts," they embody values as well. The right hand is seen as "pre-eminent"—more valuable—than the left, and at the same time, and in virtue of being pre-eminent, is taken as normal, as the standard, while left-handedness is regarded as odd or unusual. As such, the right hand represents the whole of the human body more than the left can ever hope to do.

Holism, a synonym for hierarchy

Second point: to take the view of Dumont's hierarchy is to take the view of holism, to take the sociological view (Dumont 1979a, 787). As a loyal sociologist in the Durkheimian style, Dumont believes that one should seek explanations of cultural and social realities in *social* or *holistic* terms, rather than, say, psychological ones. In our world so dominated by individualist ideology, Dumont believes that we find sociological explanations hard to sustain. The tendency is to complain about such things as Durkheim's "'oversocialized conception of man'" for example (Dumont 1979a, 799). Our tendency in a world dominated by individualist ideology is also to see society as a product of a contract or set of transactions between and among individuals, as Dumont accuses McKim Marriott of believing (Dumont 1971a, 65). Instead, Dumont seeks to grant the social level of human life an autonomy that cannot be reduced to the actions of individual agents. He would argue that the very possibility of entering into contracts

© Equinox Publishing Ltd. 2008

or securing transactions depends upon the acceptance of pre-existing values, held in common and thus shared by the parties involved. "Trust" is not
manufactured by frequency of interactions. In his classic introduction to
hierarchy as worked out in his great study of the Indian caste system,
Homo Hierarchicus, Dumont accordingly celebrates the Durkheimian
"sociological apperception" that he brings to the study of caste (Dumont
1980, 5–8). In doing so, he celebrates holism as well. Thus, in concluding his critique of Marriott's methodologically individualist position,
Dumont says,

> The conclusion I propose is that the essential question at stake here is
> about the nature of hierarchy (a value or a mechanical result) and ulti-
> mately once more about the place of values in society, about whether so-
> ciology should be holistic or individualistic, whether we should keep to, or
> transcend our current modern views... (Dumont 1971a, 66)

For Dumont, the answer is both foreordained and deeply ironic—sociology
must be *socio*logical.

How Dumont's "hierarchy" helps us understand: Buddhist monk, Buddhist layfolk

Now all this high-flown theoretical discussion should surely have made
readers hungry for some concrete examples of how Dumont's viewpoints
on hierarchy help us understand various religious realities better. Our
polemics would hardly be worth such engagement if, in fact, Dumont's
idea of hierarchy offered no help in understanding certain puzzles arising
in the study of religion (Haidt 2007). Although Dumont's major work has
been on the Indian caste system, our natural resistance to this institution
may make it less useful as a way of showing how Dumont's ideas work.
To be sure, Dumont did not shirk from using caste to demonstrate how his
idea of "hierarchy" worked. But, I am not constrained by the same agenda, and at any rate intend to bring caste into the discussion to follow on
Dumont and individualism. I thus leave Dumont to face the consequences
of his being a latter-day descendent of the Collège de Sociologie and its
will to transgress. Instead of the Hindu caste system, I shall use Theravāda
Buddhism to illustrate how Dumont's ideas about hierarchy work at their
best.

I shall argue that Dumont's theory helps us understand one of the most
paradoxical puzzles in Buddhist studies, namely the relation of Theravāda
monks to Buddhist laypeople. This puzzle is actually a cluster of puzzles.
One is how and why Buddhist layfolk persist in being devoted to Buddhism
as layfolk, when it is clear to all that the quintessence of Buddhist life is
the monastic one. One might say that being a lay Buddhist is not a *bad*

© Equinox Publishing Ltd. 2008

thing. It is just not being a fully-fledged Buddhist, so to speak. Put otherwise, the way of life of the monk and that of the layperson represent good but incompatible—contrary—ways of life, and thus values. They represent arguably good values, but values, nonetheless, that cannot be maximized simultaneously. Being a monk in the Buddhist style entails renunciation—abstinence, and not only from sexual activity, but also from economic transactions, such as trade, or political engagement, such all the acts of normal citizenship, and on top of this, often total retreat from all social life into the solitary life of the hermit. These are all practices that negate the very meaning of the life of an ordinary lay person. Were a Theravādin Buddhism monk, for example, to seek and acquire gainful employment, to consider replenishing the Sangha by starting families, and so on, they would *ipso facto cease* being monks, and simply by virtue of doing these things revert to lay status.

In their the choice of values Buddhists face options as mutually exclusive—"opposed" or "contrary"—as those we make all the time in terms of our own social values. Thus the social choice between optimizing equality or liberty is perennial and classic in our liberal democratic societies. Both liberty and equality represent arguably good values, but ones whose mutual optimization inevitably runs into perhaps impossible dilemmas of choice. One is pressed to choose to optimize one and virtually exclude each other when they conflict. This is, in effect, what happens when policies seeking to effect social equality are enforced or, equally well, when liberty is preferred. Consider the implementation of a progressive income tax rate: in order to maximize equality of "take home" income, high earner individuals are taxed and the revenues collected are redistributed to others in society, say in terms either of lower tax rates for low income earners, or certain social benefits made to them, such as free medical insurance. One effect of this, beyond a certain equalization of life circumstances for the lower income earners, is to limit the liberty of high income earning individuals to "take home" as much as they would like. Their liberty is curtailed at the expense of equality.

Buddhism faces its own hard choices between arguably good values. While it is agreed that in Buddhism as a whole, the pursuit of Nibbāna is the focal concern of Buddhists, only monks devote themselves to this goal. Lay folk do not. The pursuit of Nibbāna is superior to that of winning merit, typical of the layperson. Monks and layfolks are not, therefore, *equal*. The monk is clearly superior to the lay person. Buddhism, then, can be seen to present people with two value choices that are neither the same, nor equal, and which cannot be optimized simultaneously—either to be a monk and pursue Nibbāna, or to remain a layperson and make merit. Although it is something of a crude overstatement, there is no doubt

© Equinox Publishing Ltd. 2008

that the choice to be a monk is the right—preferred—choice to make as far as Buddhism is concerned. Willfully to remain a layperson is not the right choice to make if presented with these alternatives, any more than the choice of pursuing Nibbāna or not would be.

But what is the point to be made here with respect to our discussion of Dumont's idea of hierarchy? Buddhist monk and Buddhist lay persons are opposites or contraries in the sense that Dumont understands. I would put it that the typically Western way of dealing with such radical choices as those between liberty and equality or monkhood and the lay life *hides* the principle of hierarchy that is actually at work in the process of making these hard choices and living by them. Instead, we tend to conceal what arguably really happens in making such choices, tending rather to cast into shadow the fate of the values not chosen. In Buddhist South Asia, on the other hand, the fate of the values not chosen is well worked out because the "lower" value is encompassed within the whole of which the higher value is emblematic. There, as we will see, the ideal of being a layperson is not considered *un*buddhist, just Buddhist with a difference— and one, as we will see, that is seen as complementary in making up the whole that Buddhism is.

Quite different is what tends to be typical of the liberal West. Consider the great intellectual historian and philosopher, Isaiah Berlin, and the way he handles differences of values like the one between Buddhist monk and layperson. In several works expounding his theory of value "pluralism," Berlin has argued that life is often complicated by our being presented with choices between arguably good, but incompatible or contrary, values (Berlin 1979). These are values which cannot be simultaneously maximized. The incompatibility of Christian morality with that of ancient Rome would qualify as one such case. In Berlin's view, such value choices present real dilemmas, and in some cases, agents try to marry two opposed value systems together. But, this leads to incoherence and ruin, because the two are treated as equals and placed on the same level. These are cases, for example, where a political ruler of a state tries to govern and rule by pacific and charitable Christian values together with the values of *Realpolitik*, such as turning the other cheek, on the one side, together with power politics, on the other. Berlin, arguing through Machiavelli, claimed that this attempt to marry what are polar opposites only brings ruin because it would be essentially confusing. Wars of self-preservation cannot be fought by turning the other cheek and power politics at the same time. When would one decide which value would prevail in a certain case, rather than the other? A brutal and determined enemy will simply overpower the state that was so confused about how to practice its statecraft by seeking to exploit moments of weakness and indecision. In other cases,

© Equinox Publishing Ltd. 2008

a choice is made between values, and one is eliminated while the other embraced. Thus, in Berlin's discussion of Machiavelli, he claims that the great Florentine thinker was arguing that in governing the state one might choose *either* to do so according to Christian principles, e.g. loving kindliness, turning the other cheek and so on, *or* with respect to the harder values of power politics, such as that which prevailed in the old Roman world. There, power and calculations aimed at survival of the state in a treacherous world dominated—in short, the values exemplified in *The Prince*. If one opted to rule by Christian principles, Berlin (and Machiavelli) argued that one would surely bring ruin to one's state, just as surely as one who tried to mix the two in equal portion. Only tough-minded principles could function successfully to insure survival of the state. Christian morals may be good personal moral values, but they are only good in the domain of interpersonal relations or domestic life. Applied to statecraft, "turning the other cheek" would mean, for example, opening the state to invasion or other forms of aggression. These values would bring sure ruin to a state governed by them. Therefore, the prince must embrace the hard values of the ancients, and put away Christian values in governing the realm.

Now the point of this example and its comparison to Dumont's hierarchical way of looking at choices among values in Buddhism is to observe how sharply they are opposed in their sense of what happens both in regarding the values in the first place as equals and also to what happens when one value is rejected and the other enthroned. The point to note is that Berlin abhors a confusion of values and wishes instead to argue that choice between values often need to be made, even if the choices are unpleasant. Reluctantly, Berlin "backs into" the notion that opposed values might in some way be reconciled, but he never spells out how and by what rules this would happen. Dumont's theory of hierarchy takes on this matter of opposed values directly, and provides a theory of how they might be managed short of either confusion or radical elimination of one over the other. Unlike Dumont, reconciliation seems a residual notion in Berlin's thought world. This is not surprising, since on the whole, Berlin's effort has been to combat monism and the naive optimism of political utopianism. In pursuit of that great Cold War and anti-fascist effort, Berlin emphasizes that choosing between opposed values may often result in hard either/or choices, values which may not be reconcilable. Such "collisions of values" cannot, therefore, avoided; they often cannot be reconciled in this world, Berlin glumly tells us (Berlin 1990, 13–17).

In contrast to Berlin, Dumont's theory of hierarchy teaches that in India, at least, the encompassment of opposing values is normal, rather than residual. From his observation and study of the societies of South Asia, Dumont has concluded that exclusiveness, perhaps less than

© Equinox Publishing Ltd. 2008

monism, is the object of his concern. Dumont argues, therefore, that choices among values that seem exclusive, may on closer inspection be inclusive. Here, whether Berlin appreciates it or not, opposites are in-cluded within a scheme of hierarchy as a normal part of the way certain societies work. The lower value is neither exiled to the outer reaches, nor cast as a residuum. Rather both opposed values—higher and lower—despite there being contraries, are "encompassed" within the "business" of a larger whole.

Hierarchy as Dumont describes it seems to govern the way Theravāda Buddhism deals with the opposed values of the monk and laity, with the exclusive values of Nibbāna questing and the mundane virtuous life. There, while the values of the monk are seen as superior, the values of the laity are not excluded, but "encompassed," embraced as part of a larger whole—Buddhism as a totality. Seeking Nibbāna is Buddhism's quintessential aim, but the values of mundane lay life are not disdained absolutely. They are hierarchically relativized to value of monkhood. From the viewpoint of the Buddhist whole—from the viewpoint of Buddhism as a totality—both are necessary to the existence of the whole, although not as *equals*. Without the material and social support of the lay folk, monks would either die or be required to earn their own livelihood, reproduce themselves and so on—become lay folk! This remains true despite the fact that the values of the monk remain superior to those of the lay per-son, and are recognized by them as such. There is asymmetry between them in the same way as the right and left hand are said to be unequal or asymmetrical to one another, yet necessary in constituting the whole. Yet, the values of the lay person are not eliminated, or cast as residual. Rather, their assertion is the necessary condition for the continued exis-tence of the monastic community. Monks could not remain monks if they were required to earn gainful employment, restock their membership by marrying and producing offspring, defend and promote their interests by active political and civic engagement and so on. Monks depend upon the laity for food, for new recruits to the monastic life, for security from political predation. Were monks forced to earn their livings through gainful em-ployment, produce their own offspring, and so on, they would *ipso facto* become layfolk. And, if this were to happen, Buddhism—the whole—would cease to exist.

Hierarchy: Moral considerations

In many cases, moral considerations might be said not to apply to Dumont's asssertion of hierarchy. Rather, Dumont's idea of hierarchy is really about the place and value of *difference*—variety, complexity, con-trast, transcendence and such in our world. His argument is really the very

© Equinox Publishing Ltd. 2008

French one of "Vive la différence!" Yet, it would be coarse to overlook the obvious moral implications that might be drawn from Dumont's treatment of hierarchy, especially as this may entail a critique of equality as a fundamental guarantor of ethical social arrangements. How do Dumont's words about hierarchy bear on sensitive moral issues of our own time and place such as racial or gender *equality*? Would his very affirmation of hierarchy undermine ethical commitments to such causes as, say, racial and gender equality? Does hierarchy somehow represent a kind of moral pathology? These are troubling questions for anyone seduced by the arguments of Dumont. They need to be addressed, even if they cannot be answered definitively.

Let me say first that one might start from the viewpoint that in most cases, at least for "us," equality is the measure of morality, justice and the like. On this view, when an issue arises about "fair" or "just" treatment of individuals or groups, the right place to start would seem to be whether *equal* treatment has been meted out. Have all applicants been given a "fair" chance at winning a particular job? Have they been treated with "justice" or "equity"? The usual way satisfactory answers are judged to have been given to such questions is cite evidence of the applicants in this situation having been given *equal* chances at landing the job, at their having been treated *in the same way*, at their not having been "discriminated" against (or for), but in having been treated in the *same* way. This would seem unproblematically to make the case for the priority of equality, in the sense of sameness, as a guarantor of ethical treatment and behavior.

But, it is not always the case that equality entails "fairness," "justice" or "equity." Sometimes equality—the *same* treatment—is not equity, justice and the like. Women who attend large public events know this intimately. There, the provision of *equal* lavatory facilities—the same number of stalls as for men—does not produce fairness, as the long line of women inconvenienced by the equality of facilities will testify. Were the situation to be just, fair or equitable, the number of women's stalls would have to be greater than—unequal to—the number of men's. Thus, in some cases, it seems like justice, equity, fairness and so on requires *in*equality. Much the same logic would seem to be behind the principle of affirmative action, or even the old socialist slogan, "From each according to their abilities to each according to their needs." In all these examples, fairness, equity or justice requires abandoning equality as a simple principle for governing, much less guaranteeing, the morality of behavior. We would simply need to work much harder for a way to think about how and why our actions may be moral.

© Equinox Publishing Ltd. 2008

Chapter Three

Our Individualism and Its Religious Origins

Louis Dumont, key theorist of the individual and individualism

Unlike some thinkers who feel compelled to declare their moral alignment with the ideas they explore, Dumont generally tries to short-circuit moralizing the subjects of his writing. This is not always possible, nor perhaps even desirable—even for Dumont—but it is how he conducts himself as a scholar and author. One of Dumont's sharpest critics, Robert Parkin, put this stance in the following way. In his work on morally delicate subjects such as hierarchy or individualism, Dumont has consistently refused to strike a moralistic pose, instead

> always placing the understanding of caste before its moral evaluation. As a result, his work on both hierarchy and individualism have attracted not merely intellectual scepticism but a degree of hostility too, often on non-academic grounds. This is perhaps not entirely surprising. *Homo Hierarchicus* , which not only seeks to understand hierarchy in its own terms even suggests its necessity in the sense of its unavoidability....
>
> (Parkin 2003, 116)

Dumont's reluctance readily to moralize the notion of hierarchy by condemning it—part of the transgressive thrust of his work, as I have argued—is at the root of the irritation and outrage against Dumont expressed by such critics as Gerald Berreman, as we have noted. By the same token, Dumont's moral distancing from the equally involving notion and institution of individualism might, in some quarters, cause the same sort of impatience with Dumont's views of the genesis and function of individualism. Why is not Dumont either celebrating individualism like a classical "liberal" should or, on the other hand, why is he not condemning it like a "man of the left"? One could imagine the Durkheim of the Dreyfus Affair, in particular in his spirited defense of individualism as *the* national French value in "Individualism and the Intellectuals" feeling that Dumont was being just a

© Equinox Publishing Ltd. 2008, Unit 6, The Village, 101 Amies Street, London SW11 2JW

little too cool about such a vital institution. The Durkheim of those days felt not only that the sacredness of the human individual was so important in his day, but also that since it was so much under attack by the forces of the *revanche* that he had to lend the weight of his scholarly prestige to its defense in the public arena—hence, his intervention into the public controversies of the Dreyfus Affair. In effect, Durkheim felt that the neutrality of scientific distance was less important to protect in his own day than the sacred value of individual, and indeed the sacredness of a real concrete human individual, Captain Dreyfus (Durkheim 1975). If Dumont does not seem under quite as much pressure to defend individualism, he perhaps feels moral pressure from other quarters, such as from the need to strike a pose against what he thinks are the greater evils of his time, namely, the leveling drive of the totalitarianism of the French Stalinist left of his own milieu. If he enjoys instead the relative leisure of holding up the notion of individualism to scientific scrutiny, rather than rallying to its defense, it is perhaps because he believes that greater moral and political dangers issue from other quarters than those which threatened individualism at the end of the nineteenth century. Having said this, it would be best then to head off questions about whether Dumont thinks individualism is a good or bad "thing" right from the start. What I personally find that Dumont's explorations of individualism achieve is the creation of a pervasive sense of dis-ease and discomfort with a notion usually surrendered to the pieties of our commonplace nostrums, celebrating individualism. Dumont thus makes us "think" about the consequences of the particular set of choices we in the West have made in opting for individualist forms of social life.

In this steady awareness of the gains and losses entailed in opting for, or against, individualism, Dumont resembles no one so much as his great model, Alexis de Tocqueville. In the view of historian, Mark Lilla, the revived appreciation in our own day for Tocqueville as social seer can in large part be credited to Dumont (Lilla 2007, 46). Few other themes in the works of both Dumont and Tocqueville can be more central than individualism. Both Dumont and Tocqueville force us to see ourselves as if we were looking at strangers, and in this sense, to see ourselves anew. Tocqueville's travels through the United States in the 1830s put into sharp perspective for this French visitor just what a society built upon principles of equality and individualism looked like, especially by contrast to his post-revolutionary—indeed, counter-revolutionary—France. The passage of time from the heady days of revolutionary leveling to successive periods of *revanche* helped Tocqueville see just what had been lost and gained by the sweeping movement of radical change unleashed by the French Revolution. The counter-revolution likewise made it clear to him how often equally powerful were the forces opposed to egalitarian individualism.

© Equinox Publishing Ltd. 2008

America afforded Tocqueville that perfect comparative test case of a society affirming egalitarian individualism, but lacking the historical burdens of an *ancien regime*. It was "food for thought" on the scale of a grand banquet. For Dumont, India presented a similarly rich feast for thinking both about ourselves and others—a kind of inverted America, a Tocquevillian comparative test case of a society historically grounded in inequality and anti-individualism to pose against his own egalitarian and individualist France, now expanded to encompass the West. Following the methodological examples of Dumont and Tocqueville, we can see that, whatever the particular moral benefits of opting for the individualist alternative against the holistic, comparison will help us understand ourselves better, and perhaps be more humble about the verities of the human condition. Now, *that* kind of self-understanding, I submit, would be a good thing.

If the preceding chapter taught us nothing other than that Dumont has proposed an interesting and original idea of hierarchy, it will have taught us more than enough to ponder for a good long while. At the very least, to those studying religion in South Asia, his theory of caste, insofar as it embodies his theory of hierarchy, certainly marks him as a "key" theorist in the study of religion. Agree with Dumont or not, his prominence in debates about the nature of hierarchy cannot be gainsaid. In our own day, he has almost single-handedly provoked more intense and consequential debate and discussion about caste and "hierarchy" than any other thinker one can name in living history. The same can be said for what I believe is a second great area in which Dumont can be said to be a key thinker—individualism. Since Dumont himself cites Tocqueville with such authority on the definition of individualism, it is well worth doing the same here. In the chapter entitled, "Of Individualism in Democratic Societies," in his *Democracy in America,* Tocqueville penned these oft quoted words:

> Individualism is a novel expression, to which a novel idea has given birth. Our fathers were only acquainted with egotism. Egotism is a passionate and exaggerated love of self, which leads a man to connect everything with his own person, and to prefer himself to everything in the world. Individualism is a mature and calm feeling, which disposes each member of the community to sever himself from the mass of his fellow-creatures; and to draw apart with his family and his friends; so that, after he has thus formed a little circle of his own, he willingly leaves society at large to itself...
>
> (Tocqueville as cited in Descombes 1999, 69; 1980, 17)

Rendered in Dumont's words, individualism is a "value." It stands for the view that "every man is, in principle, an embodiment of humanity at large, and as such he is equal to every other man, and free" (Dumont 1977, 4). "Individualism," then, is that cluster of related notions made up of notions and institutions that include the human individual as a value, the modern

© Equinox Publishing Ltd. 2008

ideology of individualism, the religious institution of the world renouncer, and so on. Here, Dumont carefully distinguishes between the idea of "the individual" in two senses. First, is the individual as "the *empirical* subject of speech, thought and will, indivisible sample of the human species (which I call for analytical clarity the particular man, and which is found in all societies or cultures)." Second, is the individual as a culturally, economically, historically, politically, religiously, socially and so on "constructed" being. For an anthropologist like Dumont, the empirical "individual" matters little compared with what he believes to be our "constructions" of it. Chief among them in the West is our construction of the individual as the "dominant modern conception of man," "the individual" as "the independent, autonomous and thus (essentially) nonsocial *moral* being, as found primarily in our modern (commonsense) ideology of man and society"(Dumont 1986a, 62). No reader of the writings of Louis Dumont would doubt that individualism in the sense as the ideology articulating and celebrating the autonomy and independence of an essentially nonsocial moral being has had a special grip on the man (Dumont 1986a). Together with "hierarchy," no other notion is more important a concern for Dumont than individualism. For this reason alone, if we want to understand Dumont's most important theoretical preoccupations, and their bearing on the study of religion, we will need to get a clear idea of a number of general matters: why is Dumont concerned about individualism? What strategic purposes does his interrogation of individualism serve? How does Dumont's work on individualism compare with his investigations into hierarchy? Aside from these general, theoretical questions, a number of more specific points of inquiry about the religious dimension of Dumont's work beg for explanation, such as the relation of individualism to the religious ideal of the world renouncer in India, but also in the monastic West, the relation of individualism to the ideal of the human individual as a sacred being in the West. With the subject of individualism, we are then brought to a range of concepts and social arrangements in some respects at polar opposites from hierarchy: the human individual as a value and the ideology embodying our salient normative attitudes about the individual—individualism—have all been typically cast over against the holistic system of hierarchy that we explored in the previous chapter. Everything they are, hierarchy is not and vice versa. Where we in the West construct our world so as to value the free individual as the epitome of what it means to be human, Dumont has argued that in classical India, as well as in other similarly constituted societies, being human has been constructed essentially to mean being *in relation* with others. For "them," being human means being part of a fabric of associations and affiliations that not only makes us who we are, but is often acknowledged for serving in that role. For "us," the highest

© Equinox Publishing Ltd. 2008

value attainable for human beings is to be an individual, and as such this belief is woven into an entire ideological framework, called individualism. For Dumont, then, "we" and "they" differ at least over fundamental ideology, or fundamental ways of constructing the human world. Individualist ideology contrasts with that principle which he believes underlies societies dominated by hierarchy—holism. As we will see, individualism as "our" dominant ideology in the West has far-reaching effects, not only for how we act towards and think about ourselves and each other, but further as an infectious style of thinking or way of looking at the world that shapes the entire outlook of Western peoples even in such supposedly value-free domains such as the sciences. Some of these intrusions of individualism into our thinking scarcely break through into conventional thinking about social life, yet they are nonetheless potent for all that. There is, then, hardly another modern thinker whose work has been more far-reaching in its implications, both for and against, about the theoretical status of critical notions such as the individual or individualism than Louis Dumont (Bellah *et al.* 1985; Macfarlane 1978; Shanahan 1992; Watt 1996). Particularly pertinent to the study of religion is, naturally enough, Dumont's influential and far-reaching theory of the "world renouncer." Dumont provides us a way of conceiving the rationale of the life of withdrawal of the ascetic religious individual in its many forms, whether as Hindu *sannyāsīn*, Buddhist *bhikkhu*, Roman Catholic hermit, or Daoist sage and others too numerous to name. I would assert that no other modern thinker can compare with Dumont in what he has achieved in theorizing the nature of this most salient and disturbing example of the religious individual, the world renouncer. What is more, in the kind of dialectic style with which readers will now have begun to be accustomed, Dumont conceives of the religious renouncer *both* in tension with the larger secular community over against which the renouncer is posed, as well as in historical relation to our modern secular individual or even egoist. This is to say that in exploring Dumont's views about the world renouncer, we will also be led to return necessarily to think about hierarchy and society. Since the two exist in a kind of dialectical tension with one another, understanding one helps us understand the other. I shall then move to see how Dumont builds his case for seeing that individualism—for good or for ill—is "our" most encompassing ideological framework, and that the human individual serves as a "sacred" being for the modern West.

"Indian civilization and ourselves"

In the previous chapter, paradoxically, I promised readers to further explore Dumont's theory of caste when we arrived at the discussion of his theory of the individual. Now is the time to keep that promise. This will

© Equinox Publishing Ltd. 2008

take us along the path of Dumont's life story as he gradually shifted his research interests toward the West. In his Indian work, while Dumont is well known for his study of Hindu holism, he has also worked "the individual's" side of the dialectic between India and the West. For Dumont, this shift from hierarchy to individualism corresponds, then, to the two great phases of his career. We already know that Dumont made his greatest contributions to scholarship with his early efforts in India. He not only began his studies of Indian culture and language in the 1940s but also spent the equivalent of several years living in India itself from the 1950s. The effort of these years, of course, culminated in several works, but notably his classic on the Indian caste system, *Homo Hierarchicus* in 1966. But as early as 1959, Dumont began publishing on the Indian religious institution that he termed "world renunciation"—the separating out of particular persons from the main social body of Hindu society and its holistic ideals (Dumont 1959,1970b). The principal representative of "world renunciation" is, of course, that classic figure of Indian religious life, the "world renouncer," ascetic, monk, hermit and so on, whether in Hindu, Buddhist, Jaina, Yogic or other such traditions. For Dumont, the world renouncer's salience consisted in contradicting the spirit and logic of caste, and along with it, hierarchy. In this landmark essay, "World Renunciation in Indian Religions," Dumont argued that talking about the Hindu individual (world renouncer) required talking about the world of social relations (caste): "... the secret of Hinduism may be found in the dialogue between the Renouncer and the man-in-the-world" (Dumont 1970b, 37; 1970a, 37). In traditional India, since the individual, as the West knows it, and "on the level of life in the world... *is* not" (1970a, 42), the only way the individual in India can be conceived is in necessary relation to the world of caste, which the Renouncer—by definition—rejects (Dumont 1970b, 42). The question is how this could be the driving force behind Dumont's inquiries through his publications of the 1960s and 1970s. The lessons learned in the course of Dumont's inquiries about world renunciation left their mark on the rest of Dumont's intellectual career, as surely as had his work on caste and hierarchy in India.

Thus, in the early 1970s Dumont sat atop the world of South Asian studies. Yet, in the middle of the decade, at well over sixty years of age, he turned away from Indology entirely and started afresh. He took a radical step into what was (or at least seemed to be) a totally different domain of inquiry. He moved from ethnology and the Indian subcontinent to intellectual history and the West. While there are internal dialectical relations between these two halves of Dumont's intellectual life, this shift of intellectual focus provides a convenient way of seeing the whole of Dumont's intellectual career as a conversation between India and the West. In fact, no matter how much his thinking touched base with India, Dumont left

© Equinox Publishing Ltd. 2008

formal studies in Indology behind, never really to return, and refocused his scholarly gaze upon that singularly Western institution, the individual and its enabling ideology, individualism. This began for him a process of "reversing the perspective" of *Homo Hierarchicus*, for the purpose of "throwing light on our modern equalitarian society by contrasting it with the hierarchical society" (Dumont 1977, vii). Thus, began as well a series of works that gradually assembled a detailed account of the institutions fundamental to Western constructions of the individual. They explored matters sharply opposed to those of traditional, holistic, caste-bound India. One of Dumont's earlier efforts at placing his new direction against the backdrop of his decades of work on India was a methodological essay exposing the Western individual as an epistemological impediment to sociological comparison with India. It was aptly entitled, "The Individual as an Impediment to Sociological Comparison and Indian History" (Dumont 1970a). This essay marked the first in a series of shorter works that explored that special breed of Western individualist—*homo economicus*—along with its enabling philosophical principles, the so-called economic ideology. The first major work bringing Dumont's new orientation together in one volume was published in French as *Homo Aequalis I*. Unfortunately, the English translation of its title—*From Mandeville to Marx* (1977)—served to disguise its dialectical relation to *Homo Hierarchicus,* and thus the unity of Dumont's thought as it is set out against the radical new direction of his inquiry into Western individualism (Dumont 1977).

Dumont's investigation into Western economic thought was followed in 1982 by an important essay on the religious origins of modern individualism, "A Modified View of Our Origins: The Christian Beginnings of Modern Individualism." This piece somewhat reprised, but more importantly revamped and extended a similarly conceived piece of 1965, "The Modern Conception of the Individual: Notes on Its Genesis." In 1982, Dumont felt it necessary to develop further his views on the original causes of the "modern conception of the individual" by developing further the role of Christianity in this story (Dumont 1965,1982). In 1983, Dumont was ready to assemble these and some other related essays into his *Essais sur le individualisme: une perspective anthropologique sur l'idéologie moderne* (Dumont 1983). This was quickly translated and published in English as *Essays on Individualism: Modern Ideology in Anthropological Perspective* (Dumont 1986a). The concluding piece in this suite of writings took form in 1991 with Dumont's familiar dialectic posing of French versus German conceptions of individualism. Its title in French—*Homo Aequalis II*—was designed by Dumont to remind readers that he was working to complete a complex overarching vision first set into play with *Homo Hierarchicus,* then posed against the first moment of its opposite, *Homo Aequalis I*. In-

© Equinox Publishing Ltd. 2008

dia and hierarchy in the first moment, the West and individualism in the second—but in two parts. Sad to say again, Dumont's American publishers, the University of Chicago Press, felt it knew better the nature of the strategic unity of Dumont's work, and once more succeeded in effacing it entirely by entitling the English translation of *Homo Aequalis II* as *German Ideology: From France to Germany and Back* (Dumont 1994).

Before leaving these biographical and bibliographical considerations, it would be well to note that Dumont's shift of interests corresponds as well to a logical one. Dumont's career interests have oscillated between East to West over a common ground of hierarchy. In holistic India, Dumont peers into a mirror reflecting an inverted image of the individualist West; when Western individualism is in view, both Indian holism and its traditional form of individualism cast their shadows across Dumont's field of vision. The pattern is dialectical; the projects inseparable. Dumont gets to Western individualism by way of Hindu holism. Thus, in these writings, Dumont has shown how one might go about a comprehensive program of research on Western individualism in tension with the history of Western ideas and institutions as well as in comparison with Indian holism and world renunciation. But Dumont also shows us more: he shows us how serious engagement in another culture has pushed us to confront the way individualism as our ideology shapes the "others." Conversely, this quest after our own deep assumptions about things requires the standpoint of the "others" to help us make ourselves clear to ourselves. If this dialectic process illuminates our understanding of the individual, perhaps it can do the same for religion. So, having set the scene, let me lay out the details of Dumont's view of the individual and individualism.

Individualism: What is it?

Dumont defines individualism in both "intensional" and "extensional" ways —in terms of both how we can define the notion by reference to it *in* itself and also how we can define the notion by reference to *ex*amples of it as it takes form in concrete situations. On its intensional side, individualism is an ideology which holds up the individual as a value (Dumont 1979a, 797–798). Defined by opposition to holism, this ideology "valorizes the individual... and neglects or subordinates the social totality" (Dumont 1986a, 279; 1983, 264). On its extensional side, individualism refers to an historically emergent form of social being characteristic of the modern West, and in its own way, to the religious institution of the "world renouncer" as exemplified in classic Hinduism, Buddhism, Christianity and other religious traditions.

Dumont's intensional definition of individualism merits comment be-

© Equinox Publishing Ltd. 2008

cause it conceals a paradox. Individualism itself entails hierarchy. It does not contrast with hierarchy, but with holism. Individualism is thus just one pole of the individualism-holism axis (Dumont 1979a, 798). Hierarchy may be more obvious in holism where the social totality visibly subordinates the individual human being to it, typically by assigning social duties and ranks to individual persons and classes. But individualism too establishes an encompassing hierarchy since individualism is a *ranking* of individual human beings over the social whole for groups espousing individualism as their value. As Durkheim argued (Durkheim 1975), individualism is itself a *group* value for us in the West (Dumont 1975a). In Dumont's words,

> Religion, as an all embracing principle, has been replaced by individualism,... and individualism is thus, be it unawares, all-embracing. This statement verges on paradox, for individualism—atomism—is precisely the opposite of an embracing view.... (1971b, 33)

As such, both "individualism" *and* "holism" exemplify hierarchy because both produce an "order" resulting from a judgment of value where opposites are ranked by "reference to a whole" (Dumont 1986a, 1983, 263). Turning to Dumont's extensional definition of individualism, we see that the individual valued there names two different referents. On the face of it, "the individual" refers to (1) the "empirical subject of speech, thought, and will, an indivisible sample of mankind"; less obviously, "the individual" refers to (2) an "independent, autonomous and thus (essentially) non-social moral being...." (Dumont 1970a, 134f). Although he does not ignore the individual in the empirical sense, it is the individual in the conceptual sense which fundamentally matters for Dumont's appreciation of the ideology of individualism. This is the individual as historical and cultural—as "a mental construct, not a physical phenomenon" (Dumont 1970a, 134f). In making this distinction, Dumont means to emphasize that although there have always been empirical-physical individuals, the individual in the institutionalized moral or ideological sense only emerged in the West because of contingent cultural and historical forces. This emergence occurred for instance prominently in Christianity which "has for centuries believed in a personal immortality, guaranteed by an omnipotent and unique God come down on earth as man, apparently the first Individual, being at the same time man and the Absolute..." (Dumont 1970a, 134f). In modern times we know the successor of this individual as emergent in the value-ideal and reality of *homo economicus* or citizen-comrade— equal and at liberty as proclaimed in the Declaration of the Rights of Man and Citizen. For Dumont, it is the individual as this historically and culturally conditioned value which matters to his own program of research into our modern Western ideology of individualism.

© Equinox Publishing Ltd. 2008

Religion and individualism I: India's world renouncer

Although Dumont nowhere records his first impressions upon observing "world renouncers," Dumont may well have first been struck by this salient form of individualism in a most unlikely place—in the India he sees so dominated by values and institutitons of holism and hierarchy. There, in an India dominated by holistic conceptions of human life, whether in textual or lived contexts, nothing would stand out more to an outsider than that strange creature, the solitary religious ascetic, traditionally named the *sannyāsīn* (Dumont 1986c, 26). Thus, in a social world dominated by relationship, intense sociability and, of course, caste, the *sannyāsīn* stands out as an exceptional being because he opts out of caste and thus out of the whole vivid world of Indian sociability. The Renouncer is self-sufficient, concerned only with himself. His thought is similar to that of the modern individual but for one basic difference: we live in the social world, he lives outside it. I therefore called the Indian Renouncer an individual-outside-world (Dumont 1986c, 26).

As if to emphasize just how "outside" the world the Renouncer is, traditionally the *sannyāsīn* is technically regarded as having no caste at all, even though at one time the same person would typically have been fully encompassed in the caste arrangements of hierarchic relationship. Having no caste means that the *sannyāsīn* has lost all affiliation with any *varṇa* whatsoever—the traditional Hindu "class" made up of the familiar Brāhmin, Kṣatriya, Vaiśya or Śūdra *varṇas*. Further, his having lost class means that the *sannyāsīn* has no *jāti*—no "caste," to use the proper terminology, either. Thus, the *sannyāsīn* is neither a Brāhmin, Kṣatriya, Vaiśya or Śūdra—not a member of any *varṇa*. Nor is the *sannyāsīn* an Arora, Bunt, Nair, Nandu, Rajput, Bania or member of any of the other several thousand *varṇa* and sub-*jāti* in modern India. He is, in this way, nobody at all, since being a "somebody" is to be someone *in relation* with others. The *sannyāsīn* has cut himself off from all social relationships.

In other social terms, being a *sannyāsīn* means having dissociated himself with whatever career or non-caste social rank one might imagine. Once become a *sannyāsīn*, even the president of the republic of India would be just be one of many individuated "world renouncers." He is likewise no longer the person who once lived the life of a brother, nephew, uncle, husband, father and so on. The "world renouncer" has also "dropped out" of the traditional Indian scheme of social organization. The *sannyāsīn* has vacated all his previous social relations, and is not acknowledged as having blood relations whatsoever. His only "relations" are with his donors or devotees—those who sustain him with food and shelter, by definition temporarily, or with those who worship him and receive religious

© Equinox Publishing Ltd. 2008

instruction and counseling from him, again for measured periods of time. This same vacating of caste membership—and thus of Hinduism and non-caste social relations—applies collectively as well to the so-called heterodox Indian religious movements, Buddhism and Jainism, for example. They are entire religious *movements* defined by world renunciation. They have identified themselves as independent—individuated—from the mainstream caste organization of Hindu society by this and by rejecting Vedas as authoritative for religious life. The world renouncer movements within Hinduism emerged historically out of a religious base where world renunciation had not attained the level of a social institution, and where it seems marginal at best. At a certain point within the Brāhminical tradition, such a practice became one of the many religious options in which one might find a pious Hindu. But, whatever the innovation represented by the Brāhminical *sannyāsīn*, continuity with the previous tradition was maintained. The path of the *sannyāsīn* was formally sanctioned by the Brāhminical tradition. For the heterodox movements of Buddhism and Jainism it was quite otherwise. They neither sought nor received sanction from the Brāhminical tradition. They were outsiders from the beginning, and remained that for as long as they could. World renunciation was their entire *raison d'etre* from the outset. As such, their membership was constituted from the outset as consisting of world renouncer religious individuals. Even if they typically lived within communities of voluntary association, they neither married, nor had children, nor pursued economically defined careers or filled political offices. Except for the hermits among them, they were world renouncers who happened to live in common. Dumont argues that the collective life of these Renouncer voluntary societies might conceivably be the first instances of "what we call majority rule" (Dumont 1986c, 26). Along similar lines, Amartya Sen suggests that the ambience of these "democratic" Renouncer congregations saw the birth of the spirit of open public discussion, which has carried through its influence into modern India's lively democracy and enthusiasm for free and "argumentative" speech (Sen 2005).

But, the *sannyāsīn's* being outside the caste system does not *ipso facto* make the *sannyāsīn* an "outcaste"—a so-called "Untouchable," a member of those groups British colonial administrators called "scheduled castes." And, this, in turn, constitutes another element of their being individuals. Thus, Buddhists or Jainas are not considered "outcastes," since they have chosen individually to opt out of the entire system of caste. Similarly, Hindu *sannyāsīns*, like the heterodox renouncers, are outside the caste system by virtue of individual choice. It is not that the *sannyāsīn* never belonged to a caste or *varṇa* before having become a *sannyāsīn*. Nor was the *sannyāsīn* expelled from a *varṇa* or caste, once having belonged to one, and thus be-

© Equinox Publishing Ltd. 2008

come "out-caste." A *sannyāsīn* is both outside the caste system, but above it or rather someone who has *transcended varṇa* and *jāti* altogether. Says Dumont, "the discipline of the Renouncer by its very tolerance of worldly religion becomes additional to it. An individual religion based upon choice is added on to the religion of the group" (Dumont 1970b, 46). Indeed, as if to emphasize this remove from ordinary life, the person who later would become a *sannyāsīn* is considered dead, and gone beyond ordinary life. Likewise, Buddhists and Jainas see themselves as beyond the rules and regulations that inform caste. They, in this sense, are "dead" to Hinduism. Thus, in transcending caste, the *sannyāsīn* ought not be made out to be a rebel or critic of caste, no more than was the Buddha. As Dumont points out, the Buddha, fitting the role pattern of the *sannyāsīn* never attacked caste nor even tried to "reform" it (Dumont 1970b).

Corresponding to their independence from the caste hierarchy, the *sannyāsīn* also represents religious values reflecting that transcendence. Each of the *varṇa*s, for example, embodies a different value, yet imma-nent values—values that inhere in the world. As the laboring *varṇa*, the Śūdra represent the value of physical work that sustains life of agriculture and commerce. As the wealth producing *varṇa*, the Vaisnyas embody the value of *kāma*—that value representing the pursuit of main goals of the worldly life, such as wealth, pleasure, family, career and such. The next higher *varṇa*, the Kṣatriya, the so-called warrior *varṇa*, embodies the value of *artha*—that value representing the execution of power or the success-ful accomplishment of instrumental tasks, such as governing. Finally, the Brāhmins, the "priests" so-called, stand for the value of *dharma*, variously rendered as the value of law, lore, tradition, duty, morality and such. If one function or *varṇa* should fail to fulfill its function, the entire social edifice would be threatened. If the Kṣatriya failed to protect the realm, no wealth could be produced; if wealth and power were not exercised according to certain rules—*dharma*—trust would collapse, and with it the social whole itself. Without the physical labor of the Sudra to produce the material basis and surplus value of the whole no Vaiśya-led brokering and commercial life could happen. If the Brāhmins failed to preserve the law and traditions by which social relations were to be governed, or if they lost the respect of the other *varṇa*s, law and order would be undermined. Taken together, these *varṇa*s present a picture of the "world" in classic Brāhminical con-ception. The "world" is the product of the coordinated interaction of these four *varṇa*s in their four complementary functions. This is the "world" that the "world renouncer" renounces entirely. He simply refuses to play in this game, even though he does not condemn it or even less call it to give ac-count before a higher power, such as the prophets of the Hebrew bible, for example. The "world" is also a ritual reality, and the four *varṇa*s can be

© Equinox Publishing Ltd. 2008

seen originally to have been defined by their relationship to the focal ritual act of Brāhminism—sacrifice. Those arrayed—directly and thus physically—around the sacrifice are the Brāhmins who offer sacrifice. They need to be most "pure', since they traffic in the sacred. Those who protect the sacrifice from danger, who pay for it, and those often for whom the sacrifice is offered—the Kṣatriya—come next in line of purity and a step further from the actual sacrifical rite itself. Then, those who provide the wealth, those who are "taxed" for material support to offer sacrifice—the Vaiśya—make up a third concentric circle reaching out from the center of sacrifice, and from the ideal of purity. Finally, as far outside these concentric circles as can be, the most impure of all parts of the sacrificial "social circle" are the Śūdra, the tillers of the earth and drawers of water, who do the "dirty work" supporting the rest of the economy of sacrifice.

Now, if sacrifice is the central religious act of the system of pure and impure upon which the entire traditional logic of *varṇa* hierarchy is ultimately based, one will then naturally expect that the religion of the Renouncer will represent the *sannyāsīn's* way of opting out of sacrificial ritual. This indeed it does. The *sannyāsīn* does not perform sacrifice. The *sannyāsīn* is furthermore a person who not only has *individuated* himself from standard, traditional caste social arrangements, but someone who practices a special kind of religious discipline that is designed to culminate in the extinction of his individuality altogether. Significantly both Hindu and heterodox renouncers either reject physical ritual sacrifice or convert the real thing into a metaphor. Furthermore, the ultimate goal of their spirituality is not to feed the gods, to have communion with them, but to replace service to these social religious ends with a practice that culminates in an entirely different notion of salvation. In the Hindu tradition, this new type of salvation takes the form either of the individual soul (*ātman*) merging into the "holy power" (Brāhmin), or in recognizing its pre-existing identity with Brāhmin. Typical of this new strand of religious thinking are the famous lines from the *Chāndogya Upanishad* where mention of sacrifice is, at best, only a metaphor, and where a new kind of spiritual quest steps forward to replace the religious economy of ritual sacrifice: "This finest essence—the whole universe has it as its Self: That is the real: That is the Self: That *you* are, Śvetaketu" (*Chāndogya Upanishad* VI, viii,7). Likewise, as one of the incessant dialogues of the Bṛhadāraṇyaka Upanishad (III.4, 2) tells us, a new kind of religious specialist has arisen, with their own set of spiritual priorities—not how, when and where to perform ritual sacrifice, but how to focus the beam of individual introspection upon the meaning and identity of the self.

Ushasta Kākrāyana said: "As one might say, this is a cow, this is a horse, thus has this been explained by thee. Tell me the Brāhman which is vis-

© Equinox Publishing Ltd. 2008

ible, not invisible, the Self, who is within all."

Yajnavalkya replied: "This, thy Self, who is within all."

"Which Self, O Yajnavalkya, is within all?"

Yajnavalkya replied: "Thou couldst not see the (true) seer of sight, thou couldst not hear the (true) hearer of hearing, nor perceive the perceiver of perception, nor know the knower of knowledge. This is thy Self, who is within all. Everything also is of evil." After that Ushasta Kākrāyana held his peace.

For the heterodox religions like Buddhism, *nibbāna,* the ultimate goal literally means an "extinguishing" of the self, or at least an extinguishing of the consciousness of the conviction of the existence of an individual particular self. Thus, in the Pāli Canon's *Dīgha Nikāya* 11, 85, it says of the condition of the sage ceasing consciousness and entering into *nibbāna*:

Where consciousness is signless, boundless, all-luminous,
That's where earth, water, fire and air find no footing,
There both long and short, small and great, fair and foul,
There "name and form" are wholly destroyed.
With the cessation of consciousness this is all destroyed.

Caste man, world renouncer man and transcendence

Were Dumont to leave things at this point, his work would fall into two halves with nothing much to integrate them with each other. But, clearly, with a someone so dedicated to dialectical thinking, this is not likely to be the case. Dumont, accordingly, argues that his analyses of caste and holism form a dialectical counterpoint to his discussions of the world renouncer and individualism. "caste man"—man-in-the-world—and "world renouncer man"—"man-outside-the-world" are both "in conversation with each other," as Dumont says, but also "transcend" each other. The two operate both in relation to each other, but also on different "levels" or planes altogether. This means that in India, the world renouncer and the members of caste society are only intelligible with respect to the internal relation pertaining between each other—in the kind of ages-long dialogue with each other that constitutes, in a way, the history of religion in India. As the *Sutta Nipāta*, of the Pāli Canon puts it in verses 220–221:

These two ways of life are not the same: That of a householder supporting a wife. And one without-worldly attachments.... As a peacock never approaches the swiftness of a swan, so a householder cannot imitate a *bhikkhu*, a hermit meditating in the forest.
Between these two forms of living, then, difference rules.

But this dialogue, as with many things in India, is not a dialogue among or between *equals*. In their dialogue, the world renouncer *transcends* the man of caste. The world renouncer and his way of life encompasses and is superior to the man of caste and normal—caste—Indian life. In

© Equinox Publishing Ltd. 2008

terms of traditional Indian values, this means that the world renouncer, the "man-outside-the-world" goes beyond—"transcends"—the way of life of the Indian man-in the world. Thus, the way of life of the Indian "man-in the world" is governed by the cardinal Hindu values of *dharma*, *artha* and *kāma*—roughly translatable as social duty, exercise of power, and pursuit of enjoyments. The life of the "man-outside-the-world," on the other hand, is not governed by these cardinal Hindu values of the man-in the world, but abides instead by the values of world renunciation—by adopting a way of life that does not partake of the world of *dharma*, *artha* and *kāma*, but in a way of life that considered of higher value altogether—for example, *mokṣa*. In India, this means that while departing from engagement in caste and hierarchy, for example, the world renouncer does not *condemn* them. Paradoxically, in classic hierarchical style, and even in escaping hierarchy, the "man-outside-the-world" *hierarchizes* his way of life over the Indian man-in-the-world as superior to inferior. Thus, on the one hand, the "world" that the world renouncer renounces is specifically the domestic and social world of caste, and with it, hierarchy. In doing so, the world renouncer can be said to *transcend* the world as well. It is by renouncing hierarchy and the holism that goes with it, that the world renouncer becomes an individual—a being existing outside the conditions of the hierarchical arrangements of the world of the four *varṇa*s and the numerous *jātis*. For instance, the world renouncer is thus no husband or lover, no employer or employee, no prophet, priest or king. Likewise, he even ceases being brother, son and so on. In saying this, I am calling attention to the world renouncer's transcendence of the values of *artha* and *kāma*. In terms of *artha*, the world renouncer in general makes two things clear: he has opted out of the life of production and reproduction, of both commercial and sexual commerce. The world renouncer is thus neither one of Aristotle's *zoon politikon*—political beings—nor the consumer, "economic man," profit-maximizer and so on of modern economic thought. Nor, is he what will become even the Christian inworldly Renouncer—the worldly ascetic of Max Weber's great study of the debt of capitalism to Calvinism. The world renouncer gives up the normal human life of commercial exchange or sexual partnership, whether in the restricted realm of civic and domestic life, or even in the wider open world of temporary truck-and-barter or sexual liaisons, respectively. The world renouncer has opted out of the world governed by *artha* and *kāma*. In terms of the specific value world of religious observance, the world renouncer stands outside the regime of religious ritual, such as sacrifice and religious giving, outside the world of the worship of the gods, outside the world of merit-making for the sake of either rewards in this life, or for a higher birth in the next life. In being thus outside all these standard religious worlds and their attendant practices,

© Equinox Publishing Ltd. 2008

the world renouncer *transcends* them too. He inaugurates a wholly new form of spirituality, whether this be the pursuit of *mokṣa*, in the orthodox Hindu scheme of things—a release from the "world" of caste hierarchy and the common ends of human life, such as politics, career, commerce, family and so on. Or, if we consider the world renouncer in his heterodox form, as, say a Buddhist, he *transcends* as well all those things that make up the Hindu "world" just mentioned, as well as any local variants, such as worship of the *devatas*, and sets out on the quest for *nibbāna*. The world renouncer, whether orthodox or heterodox, puts himself thus outside the authority and domain of the Brāhmin priest in religious matters. In a passage taken from the *Dhammapāda*, the Buddha once more employs the oft used recourse to the conception of his monks as the true Brāhmins. There, he tells us that a real *sannyāsīn* in the Buddhist sense operates at a higher level than that of ordinary morality or religious duty:

> 412. Whoso herein has transcended the ties of both good and bad, who is sorrowless, stainless and pure—him do I call a Brahmana.
> (Buddharakkhita 1966, 191)

> 417. Whoso, casting off human bonds and transcending celestial ties, is wholly delivered of all bondages—him do I call a Brahmana.
> (Buddharakkhita 1966, 193)

In doing so, the Buddhist monk or world renouncer thus *transcends* the role of the Brāhmin priest, and for that matter, any other sort of "priest," such as described by scholars of Buddhism in South and Southeast Asia like Melford Spiro (Spiro 1970).

Transcending (Conventional) Dharma

In terms then of the first of the three classic Hindu ends of life, dharma, artha and *kāma*, the world renouncer's transcendence also puts him outside even the world of dharma, at least understood in the sense of conventional social duties. He is *individuated* above and beyond the realm where *dharma* holds sway. In India, this means many things, because dharma means many things. Thus, to transcend *dharma*, means that the world renouncer puts aside and—from his point of view—*transcends* his erstwile *varṇa* or *jāti-dharma*, that hierarchically arrayed set of obligations and privileges appropriate to his station in life before having renounced the world. In terms of *varṇa*, then, had the world renouncer been a Brāhmin, once he had renounced the world, he would have renounced his duty—*dharma*—to perform rituals such as sacrifice, the "sacred thread" investiture ceremony, for instance, or to adhere to statutory behaviors designed to maintain Brāhminical purity, such as avoiding the touch, sight or smell of certain defiling *varṇa*s or *jāti*s, and so on across the whole spectrum of the many, many parts of a Brāhmin's *dharma*,

© Equinox Publishing Ltd. 2008

understood as his *varṇa* obligations. Accordingly, having left the Brāhminical station, the world renouncer is under no obligation to perform Brāhminical rituals and so on—even to maintaining what had been Brāhminical purity by avoiding contact with polluting agents, such as so-called Untouchables. Notably, when a world renouncer begs his daily meals, he may well receive—and accept—otherwise polluting food offerings from Untouchables, for example. Witness to how radical is the nature of transcendence of pollution rules is the Buddha's legendary admonition, retained in the Sri Lankan tradition. There, the Buddha abjures his monks to accept without question or resistance whatever is deposited into their begging bowls—even to the extent of the grisly case of the human finger that accidently dropped into a monk's bowl. In the more lyric, and less bizarre mode of the famous "Rhinoceros Sutta" from the *Sutta Nipata* (1.3), the Buddha urges monks to cut the ties to lay society, and flee to the freedom of the new life he proposes.

> For a sociable person there are allurements;on the heels of allurement, this pain. Seeing allurement's drawback, wander alone like a rhinoceros. As a deer in the wilds, unfettered, goes for forage wherever it wants: the wise person, valuing freedom, wanders alone like a rhinoceros.

Some would argue that the Buddhist *sannyāsīn's* transcendence of traditional dharma—morality and religious duty—is so complete, in fact, that it utterly exceeds anything the paramount and indispensable obligatory religious rite of sacrifice could achieve. Thus, in the *Dhammapāda*, the Buddha underlines this novel point of view:

> 106. Though, month after month, for a hundred years one should offer sacrifices by the thousands, yet, if only for a moment, he should honour the Perfected One—that honour is, indeed, better than a century of sacrifice.
>
> 107. Though, for a hundred years, a man should tend the sacrificial fire in the forest, yet, if only for a moment he should honour the Perfected One—that honour is, indeed, better than a century of sacrifice.
>
> (Buddharakkhita 1966, 53)

But, even more challenging to us than the world renouncer's transcendence of dharma in the sense of the social roles imposed upon one by *varṇa* or caste duties is his transcendence of normal morality. The world renouncer lives by rules that often depart from and exceed dharma in the sense of *morality*—including either "our" or "their" morality. For example, one might consider the world renouncer's abandonment of family obligations as constituting an offense against conventional morality. Yet, the Indian sense of this action places it in a higher category, in some degree, *above* the morality governing domestic responsibility. In traditional India, once a man reaches a certain age he may take leave of all of his domestic obligations. This shedding of responsibility may seem to us in the West a reprehensible act of abandonment, but for traditional India it spoke of a

© Equinox Publishing Ltd. 2008

higher calling. The call of *mokṣa*, thus can be said, therefore, to trump the duties entailed in dharma. World renunciation is, in this sense, a *higher* calling, that therefore is not to be judged by everyday moral rules. The demands of *release* form the world trump those of the demands to be dutiful to the moral rules of worldly life. The world renouncer "marches to his own drummer," so to speak. As the Buddhist scripture, the *Dhammapāda*, tells us in verses 329 and 330.

> 329. If for company you cannot get a prudent friend, then, like a king who renounces a conquered kingdom or as the lone elephant in the elephant forest, you should go your way alone.
>
> 330. Better it is to live alone; there is no fellowship with a fool. Live alone and do no evil; be care-free like an elephant in the elephant sanctuary.
> (Buddharakkhita 1966, 155–156)

Or, in the more familiar refrains of the "Rhinoceros Sutta" from the *Sutta Nipata* (1.3), the Buddha—doubtless heartlessly in our view today—urges monks to cut the ties to family obligations, and flee to the freedom of his new individualist life.

> One whose mind is enmeshed in sympathy for friends and companions, neglects the true goal.
> Seeing this danger in intimacy, wander alone like a rhinoceros.
> Like spreading bamboo, entwined, is concern for offspring and spouses.
> Like a bamboo sprout, unentangling, wander alone like a rhinoceros.
> Abandoning offspring, spouse, father, mother, riches, grain, relatives, and sensual pleasures altogether, wander alone like a rhinoceros.
> Seeing radiant bracelets of gold, well-made by a smith, clinking, clashing, two on an arm, wander alone like a rhinoceros,
> [thinking:] "In the same way, if I were to live with another, there would be careless talk or abusive." Seeing this future danger, wander alone like a rhinoceros.

Renowned as well in Buddhist circles is the bodhisattva Vimalakīrti, the notorious monk who upsets the conventional morality of his time and place by transcending it. Instead of doing the conventionally dharmic thing of removing himself from temptations, he instead placed himself directly in their path in order to shift register entirely to higher planes of wisdom. Thus, says in the *Vimalakīrtinirdeśa*, it says of this contrarian world renouncer that in order to "demonstrate the evils of desire, he even entered the brothels. To establish drunkards in correct mindfulness, he entered all the cabarets" (Sangharakshita 1995, 47). While one can well understand how such conventionally un-dharmic acts seem to those of us in the West reprehensible, irresponsible and, indeed, arguably cruel and hurtful to those abandoned, we would do well to recall that we in the West have our own secular and worldly versions of the "world" renunciation of

© Equinox Publishing Ltd. 2008

the *sannyāsīn*. Young people routinely leave their parents to make their own ways in the world. Is not the pain caused parents reason enough for their children to remain close to home? We think not, because we place transcendent value upon the rights and duties of individuals to make their own ways in the world. Of course, children in our society can also be faulted for having no consideration for their parents. But, they are not faulted for making their own lives independent of their original parental units. Likewise, people called to demanding stints of public service, in effect, renounce domestic life, rationalizing this choice as a response to a "higher calling." But it is not only duty that "calls." Love does as well. Consider how in our society a member of a married couple who falls truly in love with another, and testifies to feeling an ineluctable unity with their lover is often excused the otherwise sin of unfaithfulness to the original spouse. Or, today think of the conventionally married gay man or woman with children, who "comes out" and leaves their spouse and family to cohabit with their lover. In certain circles, such a man is celebrated for his higher-order courage and integrity—an integrity and "morality" that goes beyond conventional morality. Is this really different than the way the *sannyāsīns* and *bhikkhus* can be said to follow a higher, transcendent, path? Is he not also answering what many in our culture would see as a *higher calling*—the transcendent calling to be true to oneself, despite the pain and suffering caused to others in the process? The world renouncer's transcendence of dharma is like that.

It is precisely then by these different ways in which the world renouncer transcends the values governing life-in-the-world that the world renouncer is essentially "true to himself," and hence an *individual*. In the Pāli Canon's *Sutta Nipata* (vv. 220–221), this difference is rendered in the contrast between the earth-bound peacock to the free flying swan, the monk meditating alone in the forest:

> These two ways of life are not the same:
> that of a householder supporting a wife
> and one without-worldly attachments....
> As a peacock never approaches the swiftness
> of a swan, so a householder cannot imitate a
> *bhikkhu*, a hermit meditating in the forest.
> So, in the Indian classical tradition, it has been by attaining a life-
> outside-the-world that the world renouncer becomes an individual.
> *The Dialogue between caste man and world renouncer man*

While everything Dumont asserts about the divergent natures of the man-in-the-world and the man-outside-the-world, about the transcendence of the world renouncer over the householder, remains true, there is also complementarity and their *dialogue*. Indeed, it is this cultural tension cre-

© Equinox Publishing Ltd. 2008

ated by the stark opposition of the ways of life of the world renouncer and householder that generates typically Indian forms of cultural creativity. For more than two millennia Indian society has been characterized by two complementary features: society imposes upon every person a tight interdependence which substitutes constraining relationships for the individual as we know him, but, on the other hand, there is the institution of world-renunciation which allows for the full independence of the man who chooses it. Incidentally, this man, the Renouncer, is responsible for all the innovations in religion that India has seen (Dumont 1986c, 25).

In calling attention to the function of their "complementarity," Dumont is asserting that out of differences, held in tension with each other, something good results. Opposition in India between the man-in-the-world and the man-outside-the-world does not result in a kind of "culture war" between the two as, say, it did when the Protestant reformers did what they could to abolish monasticism in those portions of Western Europe under their dominion—or when an increasingly devout French Roman Catholic monarch revoked the Edict of Nantes, thus eliminating mutual tolerance between "reformed" Christianity and the Catholicism in France. Dumont might well indict both moves by pointing out their common commitment to the attainment of a kind of purity, uniformity, and indeed, *equality* of all members of their respective realms. India, too, could have gone this way. But, India chose another path—the path of tolerance made possible by the overarching cultural value of *hierarchy*. Thus, while both poles of the opposition remains in place, and thus true to themselves, their mutual toleration (and more) of each other, has made the cultural forms distinctive of classical India possible. In one case, the prestige of the world renouncer reacts back upon the man-in-the-world and induces certain changes in that "world." Take for example the practices of non-violence or vegetarianism, both original to the man-outside-the-world and world renouncer spirituality. Ironically, the very prestige earned by the world renouncer among men-in-the-world in practicing these restrictions upon ordinary living has, in turn, caused them to be taken up by the man-in-the-world! Originally as well the spiritual value of *mokṣa* was not recognized automatically as a value in relation to the classic values of dharma, artha and kāma. In, however, recognizing *mokṣa* as a transcendent value over and about dharma, artha and kāma, the world renouncer value of *mokṣa* in a way has been incorporated precisely into the "world" it was meant to reject. These are only two of a host of practices and beliefs introduced into the mainstream of Indian religion by the world renouncer. In reciprocal fashion, the world renouncer offers services to the man-in-the-world such as offering spiritual counsel, serving as the occasion of merit-making by being the receiver of gifts and so on.

© Equinox Publishing Ltd. 2008

The origins of modern individualism

As Dumont sees the course of the history of India, the out-worldly individualism at the heart of the its religions has established a long-lived and edifying tradition of independence of its own, along with a carefully guarded "conversation" with caste society (Dumont 1965, 1977, 1986a). Thus, unlike the out-worldly individualism of the West, unlike the institutions of Christian monasticism in the West, the out-worldly individual of India never seems to have transformed his power into one that left the other-worldy religious sphere for a worldly one. Putting this viewpoint in his own words, Dumont says,

> What no Indian religion has ever fully attained and which was given from the start in Christianity is the brotherhood of love in and through Christ, and the consequent equality of all.... Sociologically speaking, the emancipation of the individual through a personal transcendence, and the union of out-worldly individuals in a community that treads on earth but has its heart in heaven, may constitute a passable formula for Christianity. (Dumont 1986c, 31)

Furthermore, the exemplary thought and behavior of the out-worldly religious individual seems never to have been generalized into a "secular" version of itself. Thus, in Dumont's view, Indian religions never witnessed the same migration of the sacred realized by Calvinism that Max Weber charted in his *Protestant Ethic and the Spirit of Capitalism*. One will recall that in his great work, Weber argued that a dramatic transformation of Western Christianity took place that in effect thrust the monastic life—and some monks too!—out into the world. One might look on this turning of the asceticism of the monk through Dumont's eyes as an *equalizing* of religious culture in the West. The opposition between worldly and religious ends disappears, as the Calvinist ideal expressed itself as a merging of the two. The tension between the in- and out-worldly collapses. There is only *one* kind or "real" Christian, and this "real" Christian wins salvation— or at least shows that one is among the elect—by tireless activity in the world, not remove from the world! Weber's Calvinists simply do not tolerate the inequalities between monks and laity, between religious specialists and "every man" so characteristic of the Roman Catholic world. Says Dumont attempting to characterize this paradoxical transformation:

> What will happen in history is that the paramount value will exert pressure on the antithetical worldly element encapsulated within it. By stages worldly life will thus be contaminated by the out-worldly element, until finally the heterogeneity of the world disappears entirely... life in the world will be thought of as entirely conformable to the supreme value; the out-worldly individual will have become the modern, inworldly individual. (1986b, 32)

All Christians are equal before God. Luther's prior assertion of the "priesthood of all believers," of course, took the first step down this path. For

© Equinox Publishing Ltd. 2008

Weber's Calvinists, the ideal of the Christian as a (this)-worldly as-cetic came to be as it never was before. In this new Calvinist image of humanity's relation to God, the one-time monastic values of asceticism were thrust out of the special reservation of the monastery, and put to work in transforming the material, secular world—all for the greater honor and glory of God. Monastic out-worldliness was simply dismissed as elitist spir-itual selfishness. It was no more than a form of indulgent escapism when the "world" was in such a needy condition before it could be returned to the Father in the last days. In Dumont's view, India never seemed drawn to the ideal of a religious this-worldly asceticism, as it had been made possible by Calvinist reconfigurations of traditional Christian religious attitudes. India was too thoroughly informed by the cultural values of hierarchy. As a general rule, one might well contest India's total domi-nance by hierarchy in the way that anthropologist, Milton Singer, might be read. Singer argued that the religion connected with the Hindu scrip-ture, the *Bhagavad Gītā,* shows a similar pattern with what Weber (and Dumont) see having happened in the West. There, Lord Krishna levels the religious playing field, and tells his devotees that anyone can attain salva-tion in part by immersing themselves in the world, but with the intention of dedicating all their earthly efforts, no matter in what domain of secular life, to the Lord himself. So, these new devotees are not set apart from "secular" society as renouncers, monks or other out-worldly individuals. They have developed a religious life, like that of Weber's worldly ascetic and defined by disciplined action in and through their worldly engagements in ordinary life (Singer 1972). Several questions remain however, such as to what extent this religious system attained a general level, given the continued existence of the tradition of the *sannyāsīn* or world renouncer, alongside the religiosity taught by the *Gītā* (how Indian!). For good or for ill, India would have to wait for the arrival of the eighteenth century Europe-ans to encounter that strange being that had gradually come to be in the West—the Western inworldly individual. Here was the "rugged" individual, the this-worldly individual cast in its many bizarre forms. These might be images learned from Christian missionaries preaching doctrines of personal salvation and the rights of the individual conscience or individual interpretation of sacred texts and so on. Or, they might have been the ide-als and practices of profit-maximizing Western traders and businessmen seeking gain for themselves alone, oblivious to the social consequences of their pursuit of wealth. So too the Indians noticed the sometimes cold and inhuman ability of Western soldiers, civil servants, government representa-tives and other political figures to sustain themselves without visible social connections—as individuals in the world. What an odd being this Westerner was! So much like a *bhikkhu* or *sannyāsīn*, but fixed instead on making their

© Equinox Publishing Ltd. 2008

way in the world of money, power and influence, when they *should* be seeking release from this life and its endless round of births and rebirths!

Indeed, if Dumont is right about the Western individual being an odd creation, then how are we to account for its rise? The oddity and singularity of the Western this-worldly individual, stood out against all that Dumont experienced in India, and thus challenged his sense of it as "normal." This encounter provided Dumont with the necessary aesthetic distance to cast the Western individual as requiring explanation. Says Dumont:

> The problem of the origins of individualism is very much how, starting from the common type of holistic societies, a new type has evolved that basically contradicts the common conception. How has the transition been possible, how can we conceive a transition between those two antithetic universes of thought, those two mutually irreconcilable ideologies? (1986b, 25)

In India Dumont had apparently got enough esthetic distance on his own Western socialization to see what an odd bunch we really are! This then set Dumont on a course of doing an archeology of the ideal of the Western individual, a task that produced the final series of essays and books of his life. Armed with these perspectives, Dumont then asked the inevitable question: how did this odd being, the Western individual, the worldly ascetic of the Weberian literature, come to be? As early as 1965, Dumont began mining the history of the West for evidence about the roots of Western individualism in an essay first published, interestingly enough from the point of view of the dialectical nature of Dumont's thinking, in *Contributions to Indian Sociology* (Dumont 1965, 1986a, ch 2). Without going into a list of details, here we find Dumont attempting to map the *history* of the genesis of the modern conception of the individual through the thought of a host of enabling thinkers. These date from relatively late in the course of the history of ideas about the individual the West with the philosophical synthesis worked out between Christian revelation and Aristotelian philosophy by Thomas Aquinas in the thirteenth century. Moving further, Dumont touches most of the expected "bases" of political thought along the way through the Renaissance, Reformation, and Enlightenment in order to show how the modern conception of the individual current today was built up piece by piece over the course of many years. This leads Dumont to carry his historical survey right through to the French Revolution's Declaration of the Rights of Man and Citizen. There, in boldly explicit terms, it notes the charter of the modern idea of the individual in Articles 1 and 2, respectively that

> "Men are born and remain free and equal in rights. Distinctions can only be founded upon common utility," and that "The aim of any political association is the preservation of the natural and imprescriptible rights of man. These rights are: liberty, property, surety and resistance to oppression." (Dumont 1986a, 92)

© Equinox Publishing Ltd. 2008

We know as well that the French Revolution acted materially to effect this ideal of a nation of equal individuals not only by abolishing noble titles, but, perhaps more importantly, by abolishing those intermediary institutions, such as the trade guilds, that stood between the solitary citizen and the state. These guilds were the bases of economic life in some ways analogous to the Indian *jātis* or castes. An individual thus was not alone in the world before the state but, like a trade union member, encompassed by his association with his guild. These guilds, in turn, bore different statuses, and thus consisted in a scheme of inequality. The French Revolution ended all this, and in doing so produced social equality and much of what passes as our idea of the *individual* citizen. Now as thorough a survey as was this 1965 essay about the history of ideas behind the rise of the modern conception of the individual, Dumont's account was about the individual as a *political* being. Put otherwise, Dumont showed how the individual gradually emancipated itself from the religious and moral constraints, and in effect, how it broke the power of the holistic structures of the medieval Christian system. This individuation of politics from the previously encompassing religious and moral values was achieved in their various ways by both Hobbes and Machiavelli, who together effected a "total break with religion and traditional philosophy." Machiavelli sought to "disentangle completely political considerations not only from the Christian religion or from any normative model, but even from (private) morality, to emancipate a practical science of politics from all extraneous fetters towards the recognition of its only goal: the *raison d'État*" (Dumont 1986a, 71). For his part, Hobbes as well excluded "any transcendent norm or value,"(Dumont 1986a, 83) as thoroughly as he reduced the social (holism) to the political by making the individual the starting point of the political process, say as an agent in a covenant or contract with other individuals (Dumont 1986a, 85).

Doubtless because he had primarily been embroiled in the details of the rise of individualism within the political domain, Dumont paid scant attention to the ways in which *economic* thinking had shaped individualist ideology. This was shortly to be remedied by Dumont's 1977 *From Mandeville to Marx: The Genesis and Triumph of Economic Ideology*. This study accomplished two tasks at the same time. It accounted for the origins of individualist ideology in the thinking of economists—of the genesis of economic *individualism*. But, it also showed how the "economic" as a category autonomous of the political came into being. As T.N. Madan neatly summarized Dumont's argued that

> speaking the language of relations..., the transition from tradition to modernity in Europe occurred when, among other changes, the primacy of the relationship of persons to one another (holism) was displaced by the primacy of the relationship of persons to things, conceived as property (individual-

© Equinox Publishing Ltd. 2008

ism). This development ultimately freed economics from the constraints of both morality and politics.... (Madan 1999, 480)

This dual move did no more than to repeat at the economic level what Dumont had just done for politics. He had shown how political ideas gave rise to *political* individualism in his discussion of the genesis of ideas of personal freedom, equality and fraternity. But Dumont also showed how the West came to regard the political as having sovereignty over the religious (Dumont 1977; 1986a). In the domain of the economic, Dumont singled out Bernard Mandeville and Adam Smith as the prime facilitating thinkers of this individuation of economics from politics and religion. To Mandeville, we owe the idea, taken from his "fable of the bees," that economics and morality are distinct and individual spheres. While taken individually, humans, like "bees" may be nasty and aggressive, nevertheless in their aggregate activity, even while pursuing their own individual selfish interests, the "bees" produce economic goods for the whole—the "honey" of human activity. Thus, it matters not for the economic good of the whole whether or not individuals seeking their self interest are morally or immorally motivated. What matters is whether in the aggregate, they build a better whole. Mandeville thought that they did. In a similar way, Adam Smith's assumption of a hidden guiding hand overseeing the individual actors in a scheme of economic transactions, freed people from worrying about the morality of their individual economic transactions. Specifically of interest to the study of religion was one of Dumont's major works in this area—the appearance in 1981 of an account of the Christian origins of the modern Western conception of the individual (Dumont 1981, English version 1982). Indeed, with this new work we can mark a certain definite turn toward an explicit commitment to the study of religion by Dumont. In having recourse to Christian and European data, it would be well to note for students of religion that Dumont has, *ipso facto*, moved well past being an area studies specialist—an "Indologist"—and has taken up with comparative study of religion, the virtual stock-in-trade of modern religious studies. To be sure, Dumont had already noted the place of religion in his first account of the genesis of the modern idea of the individual in 1965. Commenting, for instance, upon how the French Revolution had taken on a religious character, while the American had not, Dumont noted the irony of the leadership of the French Revolution's having been "helped in the formulation of the abstract rights of man by the American Puritans" (Dumont 1986a, 94). Concluding this essay of 1965 on a droll note, Dumont remarked: "Once more, Christian religion had pushed the Individual forward" (Dumont 1986a, 97). Yet, Dumont felt that there was far more to tell about the story of the vital role religion would play in the "subsequent evolution" of individualism. There, "religion has been the cardinal element" (Dumont 1986c, 24). It is now to this story that we must turn.

© Equinox Publishing Ltd. 2008

Religion and Individualism II: Origins of Modern Individualism

Despite his longstanding engagement in studies of South Asian religiously informed social organization, such as caste and world renunciation, one might still want to ask just how seriously Dumont really takes the contribution of religion—here Christianity—to the emergence of the modern conception of the individual? Is there any way in which Dumont sees religion as a distinct (enough) actor in social life, or is it always that religion is for him always only the object of the action of others? If scholarly consensus be any guide, one will note that the handful of books devoted to Dumont's thought (Celtel 2005; Khare 2006; Parkin 2003) scarcely mention the role of religion in Dumont's thinking about the individual at all! How much credit should be given to religion when Dumont himself has written so much about other available choices? Consider the work of political and economic forces that we have just reviewed. Or, what of the great cultural movements, the Renaissance, Enlightenment, or developments transforming bourgeois culture in the arts and literature, and so on (Dumont 1986a, 24)? All these considerations, would lead one to conclude that Dumont does not think much of religion as an active force in the making of civilizations. I, on the other hand, believe these assessments of Dumont's work are simply not attuned to the character of his work. I have written this book to show how very seriously he regards the role of religion in making our world, and will now proceed to show how religion attains a salience in Dumont's work that critics have failed to address.

Thus, if Dumont's own words be our guide as to his estimate of the active role of religion in forming civilizations, we will see what other critics have failed to see. Leaving aside the work on South Asia—where I would also be prepared to argue that religion is focal as well—I believe one can detect that at a certain point in Dumont's intellectual career he began to take religion very seriously as an agency of civilizational formation. In particular, this appreciation emerges with most salience in Dumont's work on the role of religon in the genesis of our idea of the individual. Thus, a decade and a half after his initial foray into the historical foundations of the modern ideal of the individual in 1965, Dumont decided that he needed to reach further back into the history of the West and to produce a "modified view of our origins," if he was properly to account for the rise of the individual in the West. What he had earlier more or less only accounted for by reference to changes in political and economic ideology alone, he now needed to complement by reference to religion, especially to Christianity in the West. The particular publication marking this re-evaluation of his viewpoint came first in 1981 in "Les origines chrétiennes de l'individualisme moderne." This was then rapidly followed by an English version on the same theme,

© Equinox Publishing Ltd. 2008

entitled "A Modified View of Our Origins: The Christian Beginnings of Modern Individualism," published in one of the leading academic journals in the study of religion in the English-speaking world, *Religion*. Subsequently this landmark piece was republished several times in English, notably appearing as "The Christian Beginnings: From the Out-worldly Individual to the Individual-in-the world" in 1986 in Dumont's own *Essays on Individualism: Modern Ideology in Anthropological Perspective* (Dumont 1986a) and in another anthology collectively edited, *The Category of the Person: Anthropology, Philosophy, History*, under its original title (Dumont 1985). Just what factors caused this sudden emphasis upon the religious roots of individualism remain unclear. Given the rapid rise of religiously based nationalisms following on the fall of Communism in 1989, Dumont's sense of the importance of religion in shaping larger cultural realities seems, at the very least, timely, if not downright prescient. Since Dumont offers little by way of personal reflection on the motives behind his scholarship, and certainly no indication of any religious affiliation or sympathies, it is not easy to say why he launched into his studies in the Christian origins of individualism. Dumont presents his work here as a necessary bit of backfilling to complete the historical sequence that his earlier studies on the genesis of the modern concept of the individual had simply left out. So, we don't really know why Dumont, a man otherwise publically indifferent to religion, in the French manner, felt so compelled to write what has become an oft reprinted discussion of the role of Christianity in the rise of the modern conception of the individual. Little turns up as well in the piece that I shall now discuss to help us answer questions about the reasons for Dumont's sudden turn to the religious roots of individualist ideology in the West.

If, as I have noted, Dumont believes that "religion has been the cardinal element" in both the establishment of Western individualism as well as its development, this must surely count as a heavy claim indeed (Dumont 1986c, 24). For an historian, as by this time Dumont now had become, the question must be to identify the first instance of something one might call the modern individual. At one point there was such a thing that one *might well* call the individual; at any earlier point, this was not possible. Naturally enough for some, we should go straight to primitive Christianity and find there everything about the individual that we have come to understand about it and everything we embrace as part of modern identity in the West. If Christianity stands for the sacredness of human life, the right for every person to full self-development of their God-given talents, the primacy of conscience and free belief, the duty to obey "God rather than man," the inviolability of the personal privacy of the individual soul, or the ideals of human liberty, it must always have been so—and always in the ways we have come to understand individualism and individual

© Equinox Publishing Ltd. 2008

rights—from the beginnings of something we could call Western Christian culture. Dumont signs on to at least part of this set of expectations. Yes, Dumont notes, "There is no doubt about the fundamental conception of man that flowed from the teaching of Christ" (Dumont 1986c, 24) and further that "something of modern individualism is present with the first Christians" (Dumont 1986c, 24). After all, what else can such biblical sayings as Luke 9:58 indicate. There, Jesus speaks of his independence and subsequent loneliness and thus, by extension, of the Christian. Jesus says, "Foxes have their holes, the birds their roosts. But the Son of Man has nowhere to lay his head." Luke also conveys Jesus' admonition to potential followers that they have to be ready to cut their ties too, especially with their traditions, even those of natural affection and family belonging: "Once when great crowds were accompanying him, he turned to them and said: 'If anyone comes to me and does not hate his father and mother, wife and children, brothers and sisters, even his own life, he cannot be a disciple of mine'" (Luke 14: 26). And, while early Christian attitudes toward slavery are open to some debate, Paul's *Letter to the Galatians* has been for some time a clarion call to human liberty and freedom: "There is no such thing as Jew and Greek, slave and freeman, male and female; for you are all one person in Christ Jesus (Gal. 3:28).

Beyond Jesus himself, and in some ways even more influential in forming our modern individualism, was the culture of the early Christians. An early Christian was "an *individual-in-relation-to-God*": and thus someone who for whom "man is in essence an out-worldly individual" (Dumont 1986c, 27). Such a Christian was the early ascetic, St. John Cassian. He seemed to believe that the pursuit of salvation required withdrawal even from the community of the wider church:

> A monk must by all means flee from women and bishops. For neither permit him, when once they have bent him to familiarity with themselves, to devote himself any longer to the quiet of his cell or to cling with most pure eye, through insight into spiritual matters, to divine theoria.
>
> (Cassian 2000, 247–248)

While it is true, as Dumont notes, that "relationship is also grounded human fellowship: Christians meet in Christ, whose members they are," the pull of individual world renunciation constitutes the stuff of a "tremendous affirmation" that takes place on a level that transcends the world of man and of social institutions, although these are also from God. The infinite worth of the individual is at the same time the disparagement, the negation in terms of value, of the world as it is: a dualism is posited, a tension is established that is constitutive of Christianity and will endure throughout history" (Dumont 1986c, 30).

© Equinox Publishing Ltd. 2008

In a similarly out-worldly vein Paul warns his fellow Christians of the dangers of the mixing of the sexes, and thus urges intense forms of modesty upon women. In a passage that should remind us that the more extreme forms of veiling in the Muslim tradition may well be rooted in Christian practice and its culture of self-denial, Paul addresses the Christians in Corinth, and rails against women baring their heads in religious contexts:

> A man who keeps his head covered when he prays or prophesies brings shame on his head; a woman, on the contrary, brings shame on her head if she prays or prophesies bareheaded: it is as bad as if her head were shaved. If a woman is not to wear a veil she might as well have her hair cut off; but if it is a disgrace for her to be cropped and shaved, then she should wear a veil. (1 Cor. 11:4–6)

More perhaps emphatic even than Paul's fierce ascetic tone are the words of Jesus that seem to have informed the hearts of early Christian ascetics. Thus, in Matthew, Jesus exceeds even the zeal for world renunciation of Paul, and with a vengeance:

> You have learned that they were told, "Do not commit adultery" But what I tell you is this: If a man looks on a woman with a lustful eye, he has already committed adultery with her in his heart.
>
> "If your right eye leads you astray, tear it out and fling it away; it is better for you to lose one part of your body than for the whole of it to be thrown into hell. And if your right hand is your undoing, cut it off and fling it away; it is better for you to lose one part of your body than for the whole of it to go to hell." (Matt. 5:27–30)

Moreover, like the Indian world renouncers, models of Christian world renunciation find ready encouragement from the Jesus of the gospels. Wealth stands equally well in the way of perfection both in Jerusalem and Banaras, as Jesus' words for the rich young man in Matthew attest. After having declared his adherence to all that Jesus had commanded him, the rich young man asked what further he needed to do to achieve perfection: "Where still do I fall short?" he plaintively asks.

> Jesus said to him: "If you wish to go the whole way, go, sell your possessions, and give to the poor, and then you will have riches in heaven; and come follow me." When the young man heard this, he went away with a heavy heart; for he was a man of great wealth. Jesus said to his disciples, "I tell you this: a rich man will find it hard to enter the kingdom of Heaven. I repeat, it is easier for a camel to pass through the eye of a needle than for a rich man to enter the kingdom of God." (Matt. 19:21–24)

Thus, the relation of these fiercely other-worldly early Christians to economic life seemed likewise more a matter of enduring what could not be changed than having a worthwhile focus of life. In the Fourth Century, the Desert Fathers represented the ideal:

© Equinox Publishing Ltd. 2008

> A brother asked a hermit, "What must I do to be saved?" He took off his clothes, and put a girdle about his loins and stretched out his hands and said, "Thus ought the monk to be: stripped naked of everything, and crucified by temptation and combat with the world." (quoted in Ward 2003, 57)

What mattered to the early Christians was not to "gain the whole world," but to save one's soul, to be in relation to God. "The individual soul receives eternal value from its filial relationship to God," as Dumont says. In this spirit, early Christians grudgingly endured life here, and were oriented through and through with an ambition to reach eternity, as demonstrated by the cult of martyrs and the rise of desert monasticism. The early Christians, and perhaps most of all the early Christian ascetics, had no stake in the state, and therefore did no politics. Their concern for the world beyond exceeded any interest in developing even some otherwise "brilliant" career or stellar literary or artistic talent. They and their lives devoted to world renunciation:

> The pleasures and riches of the world must not attract you as if they were of any use to you. Because of its pleasure the art of cooking is respected, but by rigorous fasting you should trample on that pleasure. Never have enough bread to satisfy you and do not long for wine.
>
> (quoted in Ward 2003, 27)

So St. Syncletia abjures us. So, while early Christians are really individualistic, they are a decidedly fierce and other-worldly sort of individual, so different from us. Still in all, so much of what the early Christians achieved in fashioning their other-worldly individualism has gone—albeit by a long and torturous route—into making us what we modern individualists are. The transcendent sacredness of the human person, the right for every person to full self-development, the primacy of conscience and free belief, the inviolability of personal privacy, the ideals of personal liberty. All these values making up the content of what are called "human rights," were won after long struggles, typically against institutionalized forms of Christianity such as the Roman Catholic church, as Charles Taylor among others has recently pointed out (Heft 1999, 16ff). Nonetheless, Dumont claims that, over the long run, the origins of these values can be found nowhere else but in the groundwork formed by primitive Christianity and, as we will now see, its later developments.

But, we modern individualists are not early Christians

Wisely, Dumont resists embracing the individualism of the early Christians as identical with that of the modern period and today. To his affirmation of the individualism of the early Christians, Louis Dumont immediately adds "but that it is not exactly individualism as we know it" (Dumont 1986c, 24).

© Equinox Publishing Ltd. 2008

This is to say that while our modern conception of the individual flowed from that of the early Christians, that much of the way Christians conceived of themselves would seem alien to our modern conception of the individual. Our individualism has been subject to a long, and perhaps contorted, historical development out of its beginnings in the early Christian concept "seventeen centuries of Christian history to be completed," if Dumont is right (Dumont 1986c, 24). But, what were the markers along the way of that long development? Beginning with the individualism of the early Christians, in particular, what was it in comparison with that of today? Taking these questions from the perspective of our own modern idea of the individual, at least a few points might be made. Our individualism is one comfortably at home in the material world in which we live. Many of us are, for better or for ill, rather like Max Weber's capitalist—*this*-worldly ascetics. Weber's position and arguments, of course, did not escape Dumont's notice. He is fully aware of the revolution achieved by Calvinism, and puts its achievement regarding the creation of modern individualism directly: "the Church falls by a single stroke under Calvin's inworldly individualism. The Reformation picks the fruit matured in the Church's lap" (Dumont 1986c, 59). But, what turned Western individualism toward the "inworldly" form that distinguishes our Western individualism from that of our own Western past and both India's past and present? It is not enough to cite Calvin. Dumont had to show what processes—exceptional in the West— achieved what was never achieved in India. Such a transformation, this involvement of the church in the world, of course, began in late antiquity with Constantine's declaration of Christianity as the official religion of the empire. But, this trend was deepened in later antiquity and the very early middle ages—around 500 CE—when Pope Gelasius admonished the Emperor to "bend a submissive head to the ministers of divine things and... it is from them that you must receive the means of your salvation." For Dumont, this declaration meant that while there did seem to be a separation of spheres, the mundane and the spiritual—between the king's power and the priest's authority—the priest was superior in the superior realm of the spiritual. Yes, the priest was inferior to the king in the mundane realm. But, the mundane realm was itself an inferior realm, and priest's being inferior in an inferior realm was no great burden. On the other hand, the king was inferior in the realm that *really* mattered. What is to be stressed despite this, according to Dumont, is that both realms were bound in *"hierarchical complementarity"* an unbalanced opposition in which the superior encompasses the inferior (Dumont 1985, 108). Put otherwise, "Actually the Empire culminates in the Emperor and we must understand Gelasius as saying that, if the Church is *in* the Empire with respect to worldly matters, the Empire is *in* the Church regarding things divine" (Dumont 1985, 109). Once

© Equinox Publishing Ltd. 2008

again, the flexible relationship of *"hierarchical complementarity"* is laid out. But, the move that is decisive in achieving the transition from out-worldly to inworldly individualism requires one further step. By the time of the ascendancy of Pippin as King of the Franks, the church had assumed many political functions. The pope acted in a role of supremacy and authorized the transfer of power in the kingdom of the Franks. The pope in turn acquires the papal lands in Italy, and in particular the "Republic of the Romans" (Dumont 1985, 110). For Dumont the transition is virtually complete: "With the claim to inherent right to political power, a change is introduced in the relation between the divine and the earthly: the divine now claims to rule the world through the Church, and the Church becomes inworldy in a sense it was not heretofore" (Dumont 1985, 111). The church thus does away with the flexible and nuanced relation established by Gelasius, and becomes a "spiritual monarchy." The fields of "mundane" and "spiritual" are unified, and thus flattened, since now even the "spiritual" is taken to be superior on the *mundane level*. As such, the Emperor is but a "deputy" of the pope, and not in some sort of relationship of hierarchical complementarity as earlier. "The Church now pretends to rule, directly or indirectly, the world, which means that the Christian individual is now committed to the world in an unprecedented degree" (Dumont 1985, 113). As such, the Christian individual becomes more "intensely involved in this world"—in effect becomes inworldly. The world receives its "full legitimation... together with the full transfer of the individual *into* this world" (Dumont 1985, 112). Today, given our pleasure-driven culture, we are so comfortable in being inworldly *hedonists* that Dumont's story no doubt seems strange! Nonetheless, despite our possible ignorance of the historical forces at play in both cases, we conceive our lives within the boundaries of *this* world, the world of the everyday and empirical. True, some of us live by Weber's "Protestant" ethic in living by the "work ethic," but a good number of us live by an ethic of a kind of hedonistic calculus. We are pleasure maximizers. But, in either case, we are a *this*-worldly bunch. The focus of our attention is upon daily life, politics, economics, pleasure, health, nutrition, global warming and so on—things in the world. Our individualism is likewise this-worldly or, as Dumont put it in one of his less than felicitous neologisitic ventures, "inworldly" individualism.

What then ought to be done, ought to be thought?

Where then does Dumont's exploration of individualism leave us? Where does it leave the study of religion? If Dumont's analysis of hierarchy laid bare the critical place of values in social life, and how in choosing, we inevitably put things into hierarchies, Dumont's discussion of individualism shows us just what our choice for a Western egalitarian and individualist

© Equinox Publishing Ltd. 2008

value system entails. Consider first the historical moral of Dumont's story of the growth of our modern secular individualism out of early Christian origins. Granted, this "choice" of our modern individualist way of life evolved over many centuries, and evolved as well out of conditions and institutions strange to our present-day manner of living. But, at the very least, as far as an historical thesis is concerning individualism and religion, Dumont is saying that we still retain something of the spirit of the earliest religious formations of what would become modern secular Western individualism. Take for instance the radical world renouncer's way of life. Yes, the Calvinist transvaluation of the institution of early to medieval Christian "outworldly" individualism drove asceticism out of the monasteries and into the world. But, the "inworldly" individuals that we have become retain the same single-mindedness and (often) obliviousness to normal life in the world of those severe Desert Fathers we met in the pages above. Once it is pointed out, how easy then it is to see in the image of our familiar "work-a-holics," driving themselves into excesses of the same "care-lessness" about the creature comforts of the world, especially the tendency to relegate human relationships to the pursuit of power or gain, or even to treat humans as things that can be manipulated for individual profit. Yes, the orientation of "work-a-holics" to our material world distances them from St. John Cassian or the unnamed hermit, but the same brutal pursuit of individual goals at the expense of all others binds them in a common—individualist—world view or value-system.

Beyond the historical perspective on our being certain kinds of persons that Dumont's discussion of individualism gives us, he contributes a structural understanding of what might be called our "social ontology." Dumont's view of individualism helps us understand how our society has come to accept the existence of certain categories that we assume name real objects in our cultural and social worlds. We thus assume and thus take as "natural" such fundamental constituents of human world as politics, economics, art, religion, society and so on. We also take it for granted that since these individual phenomena exist for us, they must exist for others elsewhere and at other times, too. Thus, for instance before the British anthropologist and early sponsor of Dumont's career at Oxford, E.E. Evans-Pritchard, queried the assumption of his colleagues, British Africanists blithely assumed that since "we have politics, all societies must have them." But, Dumont argues that Evans-Pritchard made a signal contribution to the epistemology of the human sciences by arguing that "there is no guarantee that, just because modern societies clearly distinguish the political dimension," that others do, and thus that "politics" would necessarily make "a good comparative dimension" (Dumont 1975a, 337). The Nuer, whom Evans-Pritchard studied for many years and at great length,

© Equinox Publishing Ltd. 2008

seem not to have an (autonomous) "politics" at all, but something like a "system of territorial groups..." (Dumont 1975a, 337). There is, says Evans-Pritchard, "order without rule... ordered anarchy" (Dumont 1975a, 336). But there is no "politics" as such in our sense.

Now precisely why we have "politics"—or analogously why we have "economics," "religion," or "art," and so on—is partly an historical question. Dumont has argued that only in relatively recent times in the West have such distinct realms emerged (at least putatively) as autonomous phenomena (Dumont 1977). Coming back to the subject of individualism, what Dumont is asserting is that his analysis of individualism also entails the historical emergence of these *individual* phenomena. The rise of economics is the rise of economic individualism, the emergence of *homo economicus*. The rise of political individualism—political parties or associations, the personal values of liberty, equality and fraternity—is what we call "politics" in the modern sense. In Dumont's view, the greatness of Evans-Pritchard's work consisted in his refusal to assume this Western individualized "politics" where it did not to exist, contrary to so much about our modern individualist way of seeing things. Says Dumont, "the pride of place usually granted to politics is due to the reintroduction, whether surreptitious or blatant, but always naive, of the modern individual into a subject where this very book [*The Nuer*] has shown us the opposite path, that of relationship." (Dumont 1975a, 342). If Dumont's work on individualism can teach us anything, then, it is to be aware of the singularity of our Western—individualist—way of thinking and being in the world. No matter how much we may wish, we carry the burden of history with us wherever we go.

The emergence and elimination of religion?

What is true of the role of individualism in shaping the emergent category of politics is, for Dumont, true of the emergence of the category of "religion" as well. This emergence, in turn, dictates a particular way to study religion in accordance with its new status as an individual. Thus when it comes to individualism and religion, Dumont does not wish to limit the subject to an exploration of religious personalism or the rise of individualism within the Western religious traditions. The study of the rise of the reform movements of the early modern period, with their promotion of personalized religious devotion, for instance, only addresses part of the impact of individualism on the way we think about religion. Dumont wants to argue that the cultural and historical forces embodied in individualism in the West have changed entire ways of looking at religion as a category of thought. Dumont comes closest to an explicit analysis of religion's emergence in his Henry Myers Lecture of 1970, "Religion, Politics, and Soci-

© Equinox Publishing Ltd. 2008

ety in the Individualistic Universe" (Dumont 1971b). Insofar as Dumont's argument in this lecture amounts to a critique of the category "religion," as generally or uncritically understood, Dumont's work resembles Wilfred Cantwell Smith's attack on a "reified" notion of religion in *The Meaning and End of Religion*. What precisely is Dumont saying here?

First, Dumont seems to be saying that religion, understood as an "autonomous"—or at least putatively so—phenomenon, is specific to the ideology of the modern Western individualism. What had been once an all-embracing and encompassing context that once guided economic, political, esthetic and social life, had now become one subordinate cultural system among others. Where religion has not become "invisible" in the sense of being particular and radically personal, it becomes one cultural "individual" alongside others in the world of cultural phenomena familiar to Western commonsense. In essence, this scenario describes Dumont's notion of secularization: cultural and social subsystems grow apart from one another, without any *a priori* or necessary relations linking them to one another. "Church" opposes "state"; "economy" stands apart from "polity"; "art" and "morality" share no common ground, and so on. Second, once emergent, the putatively autonomous subsystems enter into a kind of struggle for relative primacy, eventuating in an order of relative valuations. In our "secular" world, for example, religion is considered less important than, say, politics or economics. That is to say that politics or economic "call the shots" in secular society, not religion. Whether or not such a new ranking of values would conform to a hierarchy in Dumont's sense, would remain to be seen. The relation, say, of religion to politics might be constitute a pseudo-hierarchy in the way our bureaucratic ranking or racist ideology produce false "hierarchy" in Dumont's sense. This would be the case were religion ranked below the secular subsystems, but not given its own level of value with respect to the superior levels. Like the poor in the world according to Charles Dickens's Scrooge, religion would be scheduled for elimination as "surplus population" in modern society. Such a viewpoint is presumed by those who look on religion as being "reducible" to politics and economics—the real "base" to religion's illusory "superstructure." It ought to be added that Dumont feels that despite religion's participation in the general individualizing of cultural and social systems in modern society, religion is odd, since it, like "society" still retains traces of its archaic, pre-modern, function. Like society, religion does not "naturally" take to the individualizing and consequent segregating of cultural and social systems. Religion still "wants" to encompass the whole lot. Religion, for Dumont, still reflects "continuity with the traditional universe that remains in the modern universe." Like "society," it reflects the traditional world of holistic values, and hence does not seem to belong as properly to the new indi-

© Equinox Publishing Ltd. 2008

vidualist order in the way economic and politics do (Dumont 1971b, 33). In perhaps urgent defense of their newly won positions of prestige, radical secularists, for example, Marxists or Machiavellians, must needs insist that religion can only be approached as epiphenomenal of politics and economics. No alternative is really conceivable. As the present ferment issuing from the "religious right" suggests, religion must rule all, or else chaos rules. The essence of theocracy is that economics, politics as well as art and morality do *not* commingle as equals *alongside* religion. For them, religion can tolerate no competition for encompassing the whole. For secularists, religion's ambitions to encompass all can likewise not be tolerated. In many ways the third and final consequence of the individualist revolution on religion in the traditional sense of the great "world religions," is at once both the most damaging and ironic. The social value of individualism sought to break down the hierarchy of value anchored in the encompassing nature of the traditional religions, such as Christianity anchoring Christendom, or Islam anchoring the Caliphate and so on. In this context, individualism ("Western" individualism) arrives as a threat to the value monopolies of the traditional religions, typically as (Western) "liberalism." The irony is, however, that in so threatening the priority of value of traditional religions, individualism has itself become an encompassing value of the very same sort for modern liberal societies! This is but to say what Durkheim excitedly said in the heat of the Dreyfus Affair: for modern French society, individualism has become "the religion of today" (Durkheim, 1975, 66). It is, likewise, to repeat Dumont's earlier observation that religion,

> as an all embracing principle, has been replaced by individualism,... and individualism is thus, be it unawares, all-embracing. This statement verges on paradox, for individualism—atomism—is precisely the opposite of an embracing view.... (Dumont 1971b, 33)

For individualists, this should be deeply embarrassing: the ascendence of individualism to the status of dominant value *ipso facto* undoes the separation of independent subsystems created under the banner of secularism. Worse yet, in its attempts to dissolve holism and hierarchy, individualism as encompassing value establishes a new hierarchy (recognized or not) revealing individualism itself as the dominant collective value of our society. Individualism is required of all; traditional religion is optional! Individualism is a norm laid upon everyone; to be "religious" or to have a particular religion is a matter reserved for the sacred confines of the individual human heart. Thus in sum, the emergence of "religion" is contradicted by its own historical effects: once emergent, "religion" is subordinated to individualism or other more powerful emergent systems and sometimes even eliminated. Once subordinated or eliminated, religion is resurrected under a new guise as individualism, and proceeds to play the

© Equinox Publishing Ltd. 2008

old encompassing role "religion" played before emergence.

I trust that this chapter seeking to explain Dumont's explorations into individualism will show that his thinking carries us far beyond mere historical analyses. Indeed, I believe Dumont deserves to be considered a "key thinker" in religious studies precisely because his meditations on individualism lead us toward some of the most profound reflections about what it is to be a citizen of the West and the world, at the same time.

© Equinox Publishing Ltd. 2008

Chapter Four

The Comparative Risks of Comparison: On Not "Remaining Caged within Our Own Frame of Reference"

No comparison, no religious studies

There can be no such thing as the modern, humanistic study of religion unless it includes cross-cultural comparison of religions in its repertoire of basic practices. I thus recall more than a century's old retrieval by Friedrich Max Müller's of Goethe's classic formulation about the need for comparison in our knowledge of languages. Thus, while Goethe said that "he, who knows one language, knows none," in 1873, Max Müller would say that "he who knows only one religion, knows none." No less a figure in the study of religion than Durkheim reaffirmed the same perspective or his new science of society, noting that "Comparative sociology is not a special brand of sociology; it is sociology itself, insofar as it ceases to be purely descriptive and aspires to account for facts" (Durkheim 1982,157). In the same vein, the great British anthropologist, A.R. Radcliffe-Brown asserted that: "without systematic comparative studies, anthropology will become only historiography and ethnography" (Radcliffe-Brown 1958,110).

Among the many other reasons that Louis Dumont is a key figure in the study of religion is that he was one of our most committed and expert modern comparativists of religion. As he says of his own denominated discipline, "social anthropology," it is "comparative at heart even when it is not explicitly so" (Dumont 1977, 3). Moreover, few scholars have shown as much theoretical and practical devotion to the comparative study of religion as has Dumont over many generations of work. Fewer scholars still have made the comparative perspective on religion and culture as fundamental to what they do as Dumont. In this sense, I claim that Dumont's work is paradigmatic for anyone who wishes to undertake comparative study of religion in the most serious and consequential way possible.

© Equinox Publishing Ltd. 2008, Unit 6, The Village, 101 Amies Street, London SW11 2JW

I shall devote this chapter to showing the ways in which comparison, comparative perspectives, cross-cultural comparison and such figure fundamentally—indeed necessarily—in what Louis Dumont's scholarship in religious studies ultimately stands for (Köbben 1970, 593).

Vimalakīrti, Stalin and Mayakovsky: On being "strong" in comparative studies

I emphasize the *necessary* and *fundamental* aspects of comparison both in Dumont's work and in religious studies because without them, comparison becomes a relatively trivial operation in the study of religion. What makes Dumont interesting is that for him comparison is neither superficial nor optional, but essential to the scholarly task. In this way, Dumont takes his place alongside Goethe, Max Müller, Radcliffe-Brown and others. What each of these thinkers stands for, in effect, is the indispensability of comparison, and that comparison is necessary for understanding or explaining culture, religion or, I would submit, anything in the human realm. In so asserting the *necessity* of comparison, these thinkers, and along with them Louis Dumont, stand for what I like to call a "strong program" in comparative studies. The "strong program" is one in which comparison is not some nice little addition to the central concerns of the human sciences. A "strong program" in comparative studies is one in which comparison is essential to the achievement of the scientific ambitions of the program of study in question. One cannot simply do anything meriting being called a human *science* unless comparison is centrally involved. A comparison is "strong" if it makes a difference. One such way comparison can be said to be "strong" in the study of religion, for example, is if our assertions about religion can at least pass the "Compared to What?" test. "Is Islam a 'religion of war,' since it holds to a doctrine of jihad?" Compared to what?—Christianity, for example, with its history of crusading? "Is religion necessarily violent?" Compared to what?—nationalism, with its sorry record of military aggression? "Is not Buddhism at least a 'religion of peace'?" Compared to what?—not according to the experience of Hindu Tamils in South India and Sri Lanka. If one is going to go in for making such sweeping claims about religion, one had better be prepared with cross-cultural comparative support for them. Otherwise, one will perforce be reduced to silence. No, as we will see, there is more to what makes comparison "strong" than passing the "compared to what?" test, but that is, at least, a beginning.

Without pulling back from any of these affirmations in behalf of comparison, we should openly admit, however, that comparative studies do not stand in the highest repute. The great British anthropologist and early

© Equinox Publishing Ltd. 2008

patron of Dumont, E.E. Evans-Pritchard, was particularly, and rightly, demanding toward the use of comparison. Once, he even brushed off "comparative method" by observing that it has no particular method to it and has been practiced informally, and thus innocuously, since Aristotle. It is a "title which means little more than if one wishes to make a general statement about the nature of some institution, one has first to examine it in a number of different societies"—in effect, to pass the "compared to what?" test (Evans-Pritchard 1981, 173). Another part of the ill-repute into which comparative studies have fallen may also be due to their perceived lack of discipline and purpose. The sprawling cross-cultural comparative studies linked with nineteenth century thinkers like James Frazer came in for sharp criticism, even in their own time. In a 1903 review of Edgar Crawley's *Mystic Rose* (itself dedicated to Frazer), Durkheim ridiculed comparative method of Frazer mercilessly (Stocking 1987,173):

> One certainty finds interesting insights there. But, to a rare degree, the method lacks a critical and discriminating character. In order to prove an assertion, the author does not hesitate to gather together, without distinguishing between them, facts borrowed from the most heterogeneous societies. All the continents are scoured without order or discrimination.
>
> (Lukes 1972, 451)

Finally, anyone who has ever directed a post-graduate thesis or dissertation will have enough examples of proposals for comparative work that seem mindless, impressionistic and superficial. Do any of these seem painfully familiar? "Vimalakīrti and Stalin: Comparing Partners at Play" or "Hearts Purloined by *Différence or Différance*? Poe and Derrida Compared" or "Transgressive Whimsey or Whimsical Transgression? Comparative Tropes in the Works of Immanuel Kant and Russell McCutcheon."

The moral of these various complaints about comparative studies is that in order to put comparative studies at the center of intellectual inquiry in the humanities and human sciences, we will need to stand behind some sort of rigorous, thorough and detailed, as well as intellectually defensible program for comparison. That is to say, comparisons need to be "strong." Unless a program of comparative studies can demonstrate something like its "strength," it will, I suggest, always remain marginal to inquiry in the study of religion. To be "strong," comparisons need intellectual rigor, detailed factual bases, some sense of the rules that should guide comparison, good judgment in selecting items to compare. It is in the "strong" sense, then, that comparative study of religion becomes compelling. As a "strong comparativist" himself, Louis Dumont was committed in principle and in practice to a rigor and discipline in making comparisons, to the practice as well of detailed and thorough immersion in the factual bases of comparisons. Further, he had a great knack for selecting well-chosen

© Equinox Publishing Ltd. 2008

cases for comparison. For him, therefore, comparative work fulfills an essential feature of his scientific ambitions since it enabled him to put his hypotheses about human culture to the best test to which they might be put. This essential feature is, as we will see, that comparison facilitates the testing of hypotheses—the posing and resolving of questions of problems put by an investigator.

Sometimes, of course, when critics deny the value of comparative studies, they have had in mind the idea of the frivolous comparisons we have just discussed. But, at other times, just the mere fact of considering comparative studies as consisting in a rudimentary matching up or pairing of things is enough for critics to dismiss comparison as relatively unimportant. Even the promise of adding a "comparative perspective" to jostle our understanding may not be sufficient to mollify such critics. Behind such failure to be impressed with comparisons of this sort is, I suggest, the view that such pairings are innocuous and uncritical. After all, anything can be laid alongside any other thing, and *some*body will get *some*thing out of it. What is to be made of this subjective fact by itself alone? Nothing. Thus, the failure to be impressed by comparative work of this sort.

Taken in the abstract, there is nothing, of course, in the slightest degree wrong in doing any such simple or "weak" comparisons. Such comparisons merely are innocuous and inconsequential in themselves. They assert nothing and thus have nothing to say, nor ideally have they anything to hide—some covert assertion lurking in the shadows behind an innocuous pairing. These comparisons are "weak" because there is no logical necessity behind such instances of comparison, or even less a material necessity—at least not unless certain hidden *grounds* of such pairings is made clear or discovered. Contrary to the common reproach against such comparisons, one can then without fear "compare apples to oranges" after all—if one is doing so "weakly." But the point would be *why* one were doing so. Without a "point," it hardly matters what one compares in the case of "weak" comparisons. However, *with* a "point" guiding the comparison of apples to oranges, such a comparison might very well be "strong"—or at least "stronger" than first appears. We might, for example, be comparing the success rates of their being grown in climate zones of the country generally thought to be marginal to both. What kinds of apples or oranges have better chances of success in such marginal zones?

Returning to those feckless comparative dissertation topics, I dismiss them not because they are "weak" for lack of a thesis or point. They may well have some point to make. It might well be entertaining, amusing or even thought-provoking to pair the Buddhist sage, Vimalakīrti, over against Stalin on the matter of their comparative playfulness. Who knows? But, at least on the face of it, they seem to lack a sense of good judgment, or a

© Equinox Publishing Ltd. 2008

knack for selecting fruitful comparisons. At best, such sorts of comparative studies would be said, at the most, to be "curious," "provocative" or even possibly "interesting" and so on. Since, for example, Stalin and Vimalakīrti share no historical space, comparing them would be, at most, a formal or even impressionistic affair. No *historical* consequences, for instance, would follow from their comparison—unlike the case where a contemporary either of Stalin's or Vimalakīrti's should be introduced. In this sense, the comparison of Stalin and Vimalakīrti might justly be said to be frivolous or "flakey." This would, in part be the case, because, whatever else might be true, the comparison of Vimalakīrti to Stalin does not seem to aid in the *explanation* of anything, or offer a venue for *testing* hypotheses, nor to be *necessary* for understanding. Neither does it aspire to some sort of profundity.

By contrast, consider the difference, for example, of an explanation of the course taken by the Russian revolution if submitted to a study of comparative attitudes toward play between Stalin, and say, the Russian Futurist poet of the same period, Vladimir Mayakovsky? Both men were Georgians who made their way in the metropolitan world of revolutionary Russia; both considered themselves "artists" of a type; both were moreover committed communists, active before the revolution in subversive activities against the czar. Yet, how differently their highly consequential lives diverged after a certain point. What one should note is that this comparison immediately generates the question of how to *explain* this divergence? It enriches inquiry where the formal comparison of Vimalakīrti, over against Stalin does not. At best, this formal comparison depends totally upon the intellectual virtuosity of investigators. There is no real world "out there" to which its results corresponds. The comparison is of no use to anything one might call a social or cultural "science," such as the science of religion. In the sense in which I shall consider comparative studies, such comparisons would be seen as "weak." As I shall show, while Dumont often just seems to juxtapose one thing over against another—to do comparative studies in a "rudimentary" sense—he is, like others, actually doing so with a specific and rather pointed scientific intention. Thus, his comparisons, while they may appear weak, or "rudimentary" in form, are, in fact, "stronger" than they may at first sight seem. Dumont's comparisons are anything but amusing or frivolous, since they are integral to an entire program of cultural critique and analysis. That depends on dialectical oppositions, such as we have seen, between equality and hierarchy, or individualism and holism, and so on. From the beginning, they are meant to be part of a *scientific* enterprise, and as such, are governed by the need, both in principle and in practice, to seek rigor and discipline in making comparisons, to the practice as well of detailed and

© Equinox Publishing Ltd. 2008

thorough immersion in the factual bases of comparisons, and finally to select well-chosen cases for comparison.

Hidden "strength"

As we will see, one of the reasons that Dumont recommends himself to us is that he clearly aims to make comparison a strong feature of his study of religion. There is nothing of the frivolous or fanciful in his comparisons even when they are 'rudimentary.' By contrast, what is interesting about the history of a "strong program" in comparative studies is how it has sometimes been practiced under the cover—deliberate or not—of 'weak' versions of comparison. The classic nineteenth century comparativists, such as Frazer and Tylor may sometimes *seem* just to be heaping up apparent likenesses in a mindlessly encyclopedic way. But actually, they are also cryptically advancing theses for the purpose of explanation and proof in making their comparisons. As we will see, even when just posing things over against one another for the sake of "comparative perspective," Dumont differs from his predecessors in embracing what amount to a "strong program" in comparative studies from the outset. In this sense, he represents progress in the full and open practice and advocacy of comparative studies—even if, as we will see—he was by no means the first comparativist of religions and cultures to employ a "strong program" in "comparative studies."

A paradigm of nineteenth century comparative cultural sciences, E.B. Tylor, is just one of those who employed a so-called "comparative method" of making a "rigorous" and "strong" effort in comparative studies (Evans-Pritchard 1981, 173). Tylor, like Dumont as we will see, sought to use comparison to *explain* things in culture, even if they do so in significantly different ways. For instance, it should be borne in mind when thinking about Tylor and others like him that his method of comparison is only "strong" if certain preliminary conditions are met—ones moreover that neither Dumont nor most of us would be prepared to meet. Foremost among these conditions is the acceptance of a universal human *evolutionary* scheme of development. Next, is agreement that a particular society belongs in a *particular stage* in such an evolutionary scheme. Tylor believed that all societies moved through the same objective evolutionary levels of development, no matter where they be located. He likewise believed that strong comparisons and explanations grounded in comparisons were only possible if his evolutionary viewpoint were true. The process of explaining things by way of comparison, then, becomes something like "interpolating a graph," as Marc Bloch so well put it (Bloch 1967, 47).

Consider the following example of how Tylor explained things by such an act of "interpolation." When Tylor went to Mexico, he observed its

© Equinox Publishing Ltd. 2008

ancient pyramids and thought how reasonable it was for some thinkers to imagine that the concept of such structures had got there by means of direct influence from Egypt. Tylor wisely rejected this conclusion drawn from a "Diffusionist" view of human culture. No plausible historical links, for one thing, could be forged between Egypt and the New World. Instead, Tylor reasoned that it was more likely—it was at least worth *hypothesizing*—that the ancient Mexicans and the ancient Egyptians showed that they occupied the same or a similar *level* of cultural development. The two societies showed that they had evolved along the same route. After all, both societies had pictographic means of writing; in both societies social rank was fixed by rank, in both societies it seemed that animals were worshiped or at least figured centrally in religious life, or that the noble dead were mummified, and so on. Ancient Mexico and ancient Egypt were strongly analogous to one another as societies on similar, if not the same, levels of human cultural evolution.

Believing this, Tylor felt that this correlation between societies of the same evolutionary stage gave an investigator broad license to undertake comparisons between ancient Mexico and ancient Egypt. In doing so, we can see how Tylor's evolutionist assumptions about the shape of the world permit him to use comparison in a "strong" and, indeed, powerful way. This strength comes in large part from Tylor's use of what later, under Durkheim's direction, became the explicit principle of "concomitant variation" (Durkheim 1982, 151), furthermore something Durkheim referred to as the "supreme instrument of sociological research" (Durkheim 1982, 153). This principle entails that if we know that two societies occupied the same level of cultural evolution, we could extrapolate—predict—from what was *"known"* in one to what had been an *"unknown"* in another. We would thus be "interpolating a graph," as Bloch said. The two societies "vary" in "concomitant" ways, since there is some kind of "parallelism" or indeed, as Durkheim also put it, an "inner bond" between them (Durkheim 1982, 151). If some evidence of parallelism existed, and we knew, for example, that one had a religious priesthood, would we not be justified in looking for the same, or a similar, institution in the other? The great comparative historian, Marc Bloch refers to the benefits of such operations as offering

the possibility of filling in certain gaps in documentation by means of hypotheses based upon analogy; the opening up of new avenues of research suggested by the comparative method; above all, the explanation of a great many survivals that have up to now been incomprehensible.

(Bloch 1967, 47)

If one society used pyramids for sacrifice, might not the other? More interestingly, what do we make of the fact that in Mexico human sacrifice stood at the center of the religious cult of the Mexicans, but in Egypt

© Equinox Publishing Ltd. 2008

apparently did not, or at least, not nearly so much? Might one not *hypoth-esize*—and thus try to prove—that sacrifice was in fact more connected to pyramid building than had previously been thought? Might one not, for ex-ample, look for "survivals" of a sacrificial cult among the Egyptians connect-ed to the pyramids? Both the operations of hypothesizing and then proving are part of what I want to call "strong program" in comparative studies.

When "comparative method" shows the kind of "strength" of which it is more than capable, some sorts of religious folk resist comparison, and for good reason. Ninian Smart often would joke half seriously that "comparative study of religion tends to make one comparatively reli-gious." Using this particular kind of approach to comparison, many pio-neers in the field of comparative study of religions indeed sought—overtly or cryptically—to support certain subversive theses about the general nature of religion, and ultimately against Christianity in particular. Sir James George Frazer, Edward Burnett Tylor and other British anthropolo-gists of the day practiced what they called, somewhat imperiously, "*the* comparative method." Frazer, for instance clearly sought to argue—most-ly by hiding their intentions—that there were significant and substantial parallels between so-called "pagan" myths and Christian motifs. Frazer's comparisons were anything but random, frivolous or without serious con-sequences. To Frazer, the idea of a unique Christianity was simply false, and thus he delighted in showing how Christian religious motifs were noth-ing else than pagan ones got up in new—Christian—costume. But, he hid the full extent of his intentions. Frazer's arguments for the existence of "Pagan Christs" in the Mediterranean world was meant to argue for the thesis that Christianity had an ultimately "pagan" nature, because its historical and cultural roots were "pagan," and because in its symbolic forms, it taught nothing different from the pagan fertility religions—sacrifi-cial death followed by magical resurrection inaugurating an era of abun-dant "life." For Frazer, one could see how pagan religions shaped the very spirituality of Christianity, such as, for example, the ideal of the resurrec-tion foreshadowed in Mediterranean images of the dying and rising god, by their analogy with each other. The implications of Frazer's suggestive comparisons—hidden though they may have been—were inescapable.

But there was a double blow to Christianity from Frazer's comparisons with ancient pagan cults. For Frazer and other nineteenth century evolu-tionists, Christianity was shown to share the same crude and uncivilized character with its pagan forbears. Was it not based, after all, on the gross-est of religious rites—human sacrifice? Christianity found its "in its place" as a crude and savage thing. As a latecomer on the historical scene, Frazer and others alleged that Christianity had borrowed freely from these base and rudimentary non-Christian sources. Thus, thinking about how

© Equinox Publishing Ltd. 2008

Frazer's comparative method set out to *demonstrate* certain powerful anti-Christian arguments, one can well see why one would want to call it "strong." Even when he only "pairs" religions, his deft selection carries an implication that is hard to evade. And, although he does not feel free to lay out the destructive implications of his use of comparison, it is there nonetheless. What Frazer cannot, and does not, do—no doubt in part because he feels that he needed to hide his intentions from the threats represented by the entrenched institutional religious powers of his day—is to come out explicitly with his anti-Christian hypotheses and work through a detailed proof of them. Nonetheless, in hiding or not, Frazer's use of comparison can be regarded as an example of the "strong program" in comparative studies.

Dumont's Durkheimian legacy: The rules for comparison of societies

Unhampered by the same strict ideological commitment to cultural evolution or by the religious constraints of his day as Tylor, the sociologist Émile Durkheim was able to lay out explicitly what a "strong program" in comparative studies would be. Durkheim put together a self-conscious, coherent and defensible program of "strong" comparative studies that Dumont seems to have taken over. Thus, if we want to understand both the origins and the content of Dumont's approach to comparative studies, I believe we need to look to Durkheim. Dumont was a student of Marcel Mauss, Durkheim's closest co-worker, and learned his approach to the study of culture and society from him. Dumont represents the continuation in an unbroken line from the program Durkheim laid out by way of Mauss. While, I shall also argue as well that Dumont's commitment to comparative studies was *occasioned*, as I shall relate, by his existential encounter with India during his first extended stay there in the late 1940s, the intellectual roots are planted deeply in the Durkheimian "earth." Dumont was anything but alone in his carrying out of the Durkheimian project for a "strong program" in comparative studies. Durkheim's influence on comparative studies was extensive and uniform. It included not only anthropologists like Dumont but also the historians of the *Annales* School, especially Marc Bloch, as well as Antoine Meillet, one of the leading figures in the comparative historical phonology of Indo-European. As such, Dumont's efforts at cross-cultural comparison should be looked on as his part in the work of that great school of the study of religion and society, the Durkheimians, and ultimately to Durkheim himself.

   In their attempts to go beyond Frazer and the other nineteenth century evolutionists, Durkheim and his "team" conceived a new version of

© Equinox Publishing Ltd. 2008

a "strong program" in comparative studies. I note too that the Weberian tradition could as well demonstrate many of the same virtues and strategies as the Durkheimian (Smelser 1976, Ch.3). Nothing could be clearer about Durkheim's commitment to comparative studies than his resolve to put "strong" comparative study at the center of his entire sociological enterprise. "Comparative sociology is not a special brand of sociology," says Durkheim in his handbook of sociological method, the *Rules of Sociological Method*, "it is sociology itself, insofar as it ceases to be purely descriptive and aspires to account for facts" (Durkheim 1982, 157). These ideas for a scientific kind of comparative study seem to have become the common legacy of the entire Durkheimian movement, at least, from the *Annalists*, through Meillet, to Dumont. As such, these ideas make up what Durkheim thought were necessary for there to be a "strong program" in comparative studies.

First, as a scientific endeavor, comparative studies aim to provide explanations of social phenomena by providing "indirect experiments" necessary to test hypotheses. Comparison in the Durkheimian view was thus a long way from the fanciful or frivolous kinds of comparison we discussed earlier. It is nothing new to learn that Durkheim was committed to a science of society—to explaining and understanding cultural and social phenomena. But what must be borne in mind is that he understood this process to require the *testing of hypotheses*—even if indirectly—by experiment. This as well entailed employing the method of what Durkheim called "concomitant variation"—another way of naming Bloch's "interpolation of a graph" that we saw typical of Tylor's strongest uses of comparison (Durkheim 1982, 151; Karady 1974, 170–171; Smelser 1976, 97f). We will see later in this chapter how Dumont attempts explanation on the basis of "indirect" comparative considerations.

Next, such "indirect experiments" need to be carried out within the context of the "total social fact." This becomes clear when we reflect on how—even when he was not engaged in explicit *comparative* work, such as in *The Elementary Forms of the Religious Life*—Durkheim immersed himself in the details of the entire lives of aboriginal Australians in order to produce a rounded view of that ethnographic domain. Dumont, as well showed his commitment to the "total social fact" by commanding the religious and ethnographic literature of a great social field such as India, and also by years of fieldwork experience there incorporating data on kinship, material culture and such into his studies on caste ideology. One should not as well forget Dumont's first major effort, his study of "la Tarasque." Related to this point one might see how such an all-inclusive approach lends itself to the intense and well-chosen cases that Durkheim also recommended. Dumont's choice of Tarascon and India fall into this pattern, especially as

© Equinox Publishing Ltd. 2008

the most efficient ways to learn about ourselves. As Robert Parkin put it, Dumont "has taken more seriously than almost anyone else the old anthropological adage that the intensive study of other societies is the best way to learn something significant about one's own" (Parkin 2003, 115).

Finally, and perhaps least expectedly, Durkheim tells us that comparisons should be undertaken for the purpose tracing the *historical* development of institutions, and thus to understand our own situation better (Durkheim 1982, 157).

> To be in a position to explain the present state of the family, marriage and property, etc., we must know the origins of each and what are the primal elements from which these institutions are composed. On these points the comparative history of the great European societies could not shed much light. We must go even further back. (Durkheim 1982, 157)

Sounding like the Dumont who took us all the way back through the history of the West into the strange world of early Christianity, Durkheim seems to foreshadow some of the key work that Dumont will accomplish in his maturity. Significantly the *Annaliste* historian and Durkheimian fellow-traveler, Marc Bloch, makes the most explicit and well articulated case for the kind of historically coherent method of comparative studies practiced by Dumont and recommended by Durkheim. Contrasting his approach to comparison to the sprawling comparisons made by Frazer or Tylor, Bloch says that he advocates making a

> parallel study of societies that are at once neighboring and contemporary, exercising a constant mutual influence, exposed throughout their development to the action of the same broad causes just because they are close and contemporaneous, and owing their existence in part at least to a common origin. (Bloch 1967, 47)

While this may seem far from Dumont's comparisons of India and the West, it fits nicely his strategy in a host of works, especially in major works like *Homo Aequalis I* and *Homo Aequalis II (German Ideology),* where he poses other European world views over against Germany's. And, even in the seemingly over broad and historically discontinuous comparisons of India and the West, we might reconsider how such comparisons fit the pattern of Indo-European comparative linguistics. At any rate, we might now look concretely at Dumont as comparativist, beginning with an unlikely candidate, *La Tarasque.*

La "Civilisation" de la Tarasque et Nous: Comparison contemplated but frustrated

It is hard to know just how thoroughly infected with the spirit of comparison Dumont was in his early years, or indeed, how expert he might have

© Equinox Publishing Ltd. 2008

been when he began his career. To be sure, the Durkheimians and the historians of the *Annales* group would have provided Dumont excellent models for doing cross-cultural comparison, as I have already mentioned. Likewise, Dumont's, sometimes menial, work at the Musée National des Arts et Traditions Populaire under its director, that great sponsor of ethnographic research and documentation, Georges-Henri Rivière, doubtless shaped Dumont's outlook. But, did he follow that example successfully from the start? Did he engage intensely with a detailed case, and then put questions for testing to that case—testing that could only be done by comparison of concomitant variations, and so on?

In reference to his first major fieldwork-based book, *La Tarasque* (1951), Dumont stresses the narrowness of his first struggles with ethnology in the Provençal town of Tarascon just after his release from a prisoner of war camp in World War II. Dumont describes *La Tarasque* as a merely descriptive study of the festival of the Rhone River monster, "La Tarasque." Yet, it is hard to imagine his being either ignorant or totally insulated from the bolder theoretical influences of the Durkheimians or the *Annalistes* (Dumont 1951). Yet, if we are to trust the end result of his work in Provençe, Dumont seems to have ignored theoretical and comparative approaches. Is not *La Tarasque* subtitled "A Descriptive Essay of a Local Fact from an Ethnographic Point of View," after all? Explaining himself in an interview first published in *Le Monde Dimanche* (1981), Dumont observes of this early work:

> It's a strange book. A sort of huge descriptive chart which would never have been published but for the imagination of Jean Paulhan. Anthropologists have turned away so much, especially the Anglo-Saxons, from the detailed description which everything should begin with, that it is reassuring for me to learn time to time that young people refer to it and cite it. It's perhaps a demonstration of the virtue of detail. (Delacampagne 1981, 4)

Yet, as Dumont goes on to explain the character of this work further, we see the once and future comparativist emerging more clearly. For one thing, the myths and ritual of "La Tarasque" were never to be studied in splendid isolation, says Dumont. They were to be studied *alongside—comparare* (Latin)—other relevant items of a larger context, in this case dragon symbolism and mythology. This project took its rise during Dumont's time as a prisoner of war in Germany. There, Dumont tells us that he had become interested in the symbolism of dragons, and that he had started an "Indo-European comparison of them" (Galey 1982, 14). After the war, Dumont was encouraged in this interest with perhaps the most qualified person in the world to advise him—Professor Georges Dumézil, the dean of comparative studies of Indo-European mythology and symbolism. Dumézil urged Dumont to proceed cautiously and to work first on a

© Equinox Publishing Ltd. 2008

monograph. In time, under the direction of Rivière, the monograph was to become, *La Tarasque* (Galey 1982, 14).

Thus, far from the first impressions one gets of Dumont's work in Tarascon, he originally had comparativist ambitions in doing his study of the ritual and cult of the river monster, "La Tarasque," and of her defeat at the hands of Saint Martha. Explaining his eminently comparative perspective as it continued to develop as he worked in Tarascon, Dumont tells us, "It's very simple," referring to the comparative strategy he had finally envisioned: "the town and region of Tarascon stand out there within a larger unit, let us say, Mediterranean Christianity, and with reference to that whole. It's what I have called Parson's Law: the first determination of a sub-system is found in its relation to the system it is part of"(Delacampagne 1981, 4). So, what then stopped Dumont from realizing this perfectly plain sketch of a comparative project? "The author was then incapable of it," he tells us in a staggering piece of self-effacing humility! He just was not up to the task that his vision for studying "La Tarasque" demanded.

India and the West: One thing (deliberately) set alongside another

So, Dumont's full embrace of comparativism and a successful execution of such a project would have to wait until 1948, when he began his Indian fieldwork and writing. There, from the beginning, Dumont tells us that he

> had comparison very much in mind, and from that point of view I was quickly rewarded beyond expectation. But the initial intention was that the study should be as detailed as the previous one [*La Tarasque*]. It turned out otherwise mainly, I think, because, once assured of the sociological unity of India, I was caught—I was, so to speak, sucked into a whirlwind of more and more general questions, about renunciation, about kingship or dominance, about caste and finally about modern ideology in the West... which absorbed my time and distracted me from writing up in detail the results of my north Indian field work. (Galey 1982, 20)

And, so in this way, a fully blown comparativist *and* theoretical thinker were born in the same instant, in part because India forced Dumont to pose "questions"—to pose hypotheses that demanded testing and solution. In effect, Dumont was putting himself in the position to engage a "strong program" in comparative study.

Critical to Dumont's coming round to the cause of "strong" comparison must have been his good faith encounter with novelty, *difference*, with relative unknowns—even as these encounters with the other should eventually lead him back to the West. Dumont's orientation to difference also nicely puts Dumont in league with his intellectual kin among fellow-trav-

© Equinox Publishing Ltd. 2008

elers of the Durkheimians, such as the linguist Antoine Meillet and the historian Marc Bloch. Citing Meillet in this regard, Bloch observed

> Not long ago, at the beginning of a work intended to mark the specific elements in the development of the Germanic languages as compared with the other Indo-Germanic languages, Meillet put forward as one of the essential tasks for comparative linguistics a sustained attempt to "show the originality of the different languages." In the same way comparative history has a duty to bring out the "originality" of the different societies.
>
> (Bloch 1967, 58)

Speaking of those first periods in his encounter with the Indian "other," Dumont says that

> comparison had always been there, in intention: to learn something about ourselves while studying other people. In this way, Dumont began from within a small region [Dumont's book, *Hierarchy and Marriage Alliance*] to comparison between north and south, and finally between India and the West. (Galey 1982, 21)

Thus, when I first took in a cricket match as graduate student in England so much of what I saw was "known"—was the same (or similar enough) as baseball: a leisurely summer's game, marked out in "innings," played on a carpet of turf, players uniformed in loose fitting white trousers and open collar shirts, the batting of a ball tossed ("bowled") overhand, the "outs" made by catching a batted ball, the mad dash between "wickets" to accumulate "runs," or the maximum score for batting a ball out of the playing field—hitting for a "six"—seemed like the "home runs" one knows well from the American sport. Yet, how different the two sports are, how much of what was going on was relatively unknown to me at the time, even as it is argued that cricket was baseball's ancient ancestor (with apologies to "rounders"): baseball's nine innings to crickets' maximum of two, baseball's "pitching"—bent elbow required—of the ball directly into the catcher's mitt, contrasted to cricket's general practice of "bowling"—bent elbow forbidden—the ball stiff armed and on the bounce into the "wicket keeper's" mitt, and so on. Without claiming more, let me only reiterate the how encounters with difference such as Dumont experienced, where we might reasonably expect similarity, seemed to spur comparison in the rudimentary form of matching the newly encountered with our previous expectations. Similarly, when Dumont, thus, saw something different— especially where he might first detect or expect to find similarity or identity—his inquisitive mind laid the unknown alongside the known. His inquisitive mind matched up known and unknown to see how they "compared." Given time, the questions would come and the hypotheses posed for the sake of testing. What we have in Dumont's works on caste, hierarchy,

© Equinox Publishing Ltd. 2008

individualism, world renunciation and such are the products of that questioning and the formation of hypotheses ready-made for testing.

Thus, something like my experience with cricket in England seems to have marked Dumont's early encounters with India. There, one of the first lessons Dumont learned was to become persuaded of that reality of *difference*. In conversation, Dumont, recalled how uncomfortable his wife and he felt when on their first fieldwork stint in India. They went to India full of liberal goodwill and tolerant benevolence. He wanted no special fuss to be made over him or his wife. He sought no privileges—especially in the waning days of Western colonialism in the subcontinent. He wanted only to be treated as an equal—to be received on the same level as the Indians—as their equals. He sought, moreover, a kind of easy familiarity with his hosts, a kind of intimacy of human fellowship with them—indeed, all the sorts of well-meaning things socially-conscious "post-colonial" progressives would want. But the Indians had other ideas. The "Others" have a way of surprising us: that's *why* they are "other." The Indian "Others" were playing another kind of "game"—as different perhaps as cricket was from baseball. They confounded the liberal goodwill and tolerant humanistic intentions of the Dumonts by expecting them to behave like members of an exalted group, like members of a superior class of people. Nothing disappointed the Indians more than when the Dumonts treated the Indians as equals and when they demanded to be treated as equals by the Indians. In effect, their Indian hosts saw the Dumonts hierarchically, not egalitarily, and were confused, if not somewhat offended, when the Dumonts initiated contact by playing the social "game" by another—egalitarian—set of rules. Becoming convinced that others see the world and act in it often according to very different rules and values is often not so easy to do. We enter another culture often with the best intentions of how to treat our hosts. The problem is that what is "best" in our eyes sometimes differs diametrically from what is "best" in theirs. In a nutshell, this is what Dumont learned by first-hand experience of questioning induced by an encounter with difference.

This experience of difference, of course, proved to be very frustrating for Dumont. But, overcoming his frustration, he learned a valuable lesson—namely something vital that Indian society was trying to teach these well-meaning Westerners about itself. As it inevitably happened—since comparison involves a dialectical aspect, as we will see—Dumont learned something about himself as well, that is to say, about himself as a Westerner. This was a great lesson about difference. In effect, it was not until Dumont grasped that he had encountered something "other"—something different and relatively unknown—that he needed to take stock of these differences as well as of the similarities. This is also to say that Dumont came to see that comparison was in order. Two societies, although similar in

© Equinox Publishing Ltd. 2008

many ways, differed. These similarities and differences had to be matched up against one another—they had to be *paired* up over against each other: they called out for *comparison*, since the facts of difference demanded answers. "Why were things like this, and not some other way?"

Thus, once Dumont let this reality of difference sink into him and shape him, he apparently was utterly changed. Encountering difference as real, meant that honest comparison and challenge to one's own way of looking at the world and acting in it were in order. Not to overdramatize this example, but even if Dumont had always been aware intellectually of how moderns differed from others, of how the West was not to be taken as the measure of "the rest," when it came to a lived existential situation, he found it too easy to fall into comfortable assumptions about the common humanity of all peoples. This assumption was, of course, a feature of Dumont's own Western Enlightenment world view, and thus a factor in his playing down the difference he met in India. Thus, as a well-meaning liberal internationalist visiting India, Dumont seemed—whether consciously or not—prone to flatten out relationships with others in perhaps an understandable assumption of a common, universal humanity. But, this assimilation of the other into oneself meant that Dumont did not compare, since one only compares with that which is something one can "pair" with oneself—with something that is not identical with oneself, even if it may resemble oneself. Appreciating difference, then, was the way Dumont took the first step toward appreciating the need to compare. But, where in all this encounter with difference, is the element of *risk* about which I mentioned in the beginning?

Confrontation with an "other"—especially one that represented the long history of a great civilization like India's—inevitably brought with it a challenge. It brought a series of deep questions. In turn, these provoked the formation of hypotheses formed in order to explain difference. It was as if the Indians were putting a challenge to Dumont, "Why do you persist in doing things as you do when, as you can see here in India, things can be done otherwise?" What I find great in Dumont is that his work, in effect, represents the willingness to take up this challenge, and to put at risk our way of doing things. What Dumont puts at risk are nothing less than our own Western notions and fundamental categories by asking questions about the fundamental grounds of the way we, and the Indians, are. He is again, as I have argued all along, a far more disruptive or "transgressive" a thinker than usually regarded. Here, he now shows that even beyond arguing the case for so popularly disagreeable a notion as hierarchy, he proposes that his comparative methodology be put to the service of potentially upsetting our ordinary ways of thinking. All of, or most of, this way of proceeding began for Dumont in India—something the previous

© Equinox Publishing Ltd. 2008

two chapters, with their constant comparative reflection between India and the West—surely already have suggested.

Comparison and risk: Dumont, serial transgressor

Yet, despite Dumont's impeccable Durkheimian lineage, I have been arguing all along that in some ways Dumont fits better with the style of a later generation of Durkheimians than Durkheim himself. In terms of brute chronology, Dumont fits in somewhere between the generation of Bataille, Bloch and Callois over against the generation of Durkheim. True, like Durkheim, Dumont has been one of our greatest theoretical champions and accomplished practitioners of cross-cultural comparison in the study of religion. And true again, like Durkheim, for Dumont, cross-cultural comparison has been a prime vehicle for understanding both others and ourselves. In that sense, comparison is really about a Dumontian anthropology ready-made for cross-cultural comparative study.

These historical and intellectual considerations notwithstanding, it is seldom appreciated that Dumont's comparative perspective is essentially conditioned by a moral attitude of *courage and risk*. Thus, comparison for Dumont is not only something intellectual, but a matter of larger human concerns that, in turn, colors his whole outlook on life. For Dumont, comparison is no idle or merely intellectual pastime; it is an activity that places our entire way of looking at the world to the fore and likewise other ways of seeing the world into question. This is so, as I shall now argue, because Dumont's program of cross-cultural comparison seeks not only to be a tool for understanding the world, but also a way of changing it. It not only changes our ordinary way of seeing things, but also seeks to change the way the social science profession carries on its business of cross-cultural comparative study. Dumont sees comparative study fundamentally as an operation that entails us to risk some of those things that we would otherwise seek to protect. This is why Dumont can speak, for example, as wanting to press a program of comparative study of religion and culture because it would work to prevent our "remaining caged within our own frame of reference" (Dumont 1975b, 153). Dumont wants us all to liberate ourselves from the confines of our own world views. But, to anyone who has tried to leave the security of one's own beliefs and values, comparison *can* be a "risky proposition."

I realize that until now I have played down the "strength" of the rudimentary sense of comparing as the English "compare" literally meaning to "match" or to "pair"—from the Latin "*comparare*." The purpose of playing down comparison as "pairing" was to underline how much more there is to comparison than that. Having established this point, we can now

© Equinox Publishing Ltd. 2008

go on and explore how even this simple or rudimentary form of comparison can attain a level of "strength" perhaps unappreciated. There are at least two ways we can see how even simple comparisons can gain some "strength."

First, comparison in a relatively rudimentary sense can fulfill useful functions for creative thinking. When things are paired, when they are set into comparative perspective—one may have no particular agendas or purposes in mind. Rather than offering threats to uniqueness as Chantepie de la Saussaye imagined, some instances of such pairings are simply "good to think" in the Lévi-Straussian sense. The mere whiff of a suggestion that common class membership may be in mind may rouse thought, even when no particular purpose for doing so may be in mind, or when no particular hypothesis is being tested. This is altogether salutary for stimulating thinking, and although it may not be comparison at its most powerful, it is useful all the same. For example, while one may pair the engagement of the United States in Iraq with other foreign military engagements, some may be more suggestive than others. Does it, for example, provoke more consequential thought to be paired with the USA in Viet Nam, or the French in Algeria, or the Israelis in southern Lebanon? Each pairing carries with it a whole series of interesting implications, extended analogies or differences, and further openings for thought without committing one to a particular conclusion or hypothesis. Thus a *comparative perspective* can be a delightfully *heuristic*, because comparison energizes our imaginations—without necessarily determining the direction or outcome of such thinking.

Second, sometimes, depending on the context, even such innocuous forms of comparison can seem subversive to conventional ways of thinking. In this way, a comparison can gain a kind of "strength" by having a hidden thesis or hypothesis attributed to it. It can then become risky merely to put some notions alongside others, because they are not in fact innocuous or innocent, but "loaded." This is so especially, as I said earlier, when for polemical reasons a thinkers' proposing a comparison will secret some idea, thesis and such behind what ordinarily would appear to be an innocent laying of one thing alongside another. A common suspicion of such a *hidden* thesis is that in pairing two things, we may—often at least implicitly—insinuate that the two notions are members of the *same class*. Despite the fact that this is may be false, and not intentional, one may be saying that the two things are *like* each other.

Historically, in the study of religion, the assumption that comparison concealed a hidden agenda of promoting religious likeness or shared class membership has held up progress in our field. Some believers might feel that their "religion" is true and unique, while the others are just false

© Equinox Publishing Ltd. 2008

"superstitions" or non-religious "philosophies." In this case, simply by creating the terms "superstitions" or "philosophies" and labeling what to others might be called a "religion," the exclusive believer rules these other "religions" out of court from the start. So, even when someone making comparative studies does not *intend* to make such a "strong" claim, even when they might only seek to lay, say, Christianity alongside Buddhism or Islam for the sake of formal inspection, such rudimentary comparison can have "strength" *imputed* to it.

Accordingly, I have argued that the *perceived* threat of comparative studies is one of the main reasons why some believing Christian folk have stood against religious studies or comparative study of religions (Strenski 2005). They object even to the most innocent pairing—comparison—of one religion to another because they believe their Christianity to be unique—and thus *incomparable*. One such case involved a spokesperson for a Christian denomination who denied that Yahweh and Allah were the same as God. Something of the same tendency has been seen in Pope Benedict XVI's attacks on Islam as holding to an idea of God that ill fits the Christian one. This sort of believer, thus, takes the very act of comparing "religions" or "gods" to imply the *veridical religious equality* of the religions in question—or at the very least *equality* insofar as their common membership in a class that includes both religions are members. To some, even the mere *implication* of common class membership diminishes the unique value of their religion in the process. So, they resist. They refuse to *risk* comparison. Such scruples were precisely why one of the first phenomenologists of religion, the pious Christian, Chantepie de la Saussaye, omitted Christianity from his pioneering *Manual of the History of Religions* (Chantepie de la Saussaye 1897; Hubert 1904). Doubtless as well Karl Barth's distinction between the Word and the "religion" of Christianity rests on the same foundations.

Now, two points ought to be made about the lamentable situation in which even rudimentary comparisons are assumed to imply the thesis of likeness. First, of course, as I have already mentioned, is that likeness is not necessarily implied in making comparisons at all, and thus no necessary "strength" can be credited such simply pairings. Second, but if one *wants* to make such simple comparisons have "strength," then there are ways to do so—by either explicitly or secretly selecting items for comparison that make implied claims by virtue of their context. "Shall I compare thee to a summer's day?" says Shakespeare in Sonnet 18—meaning full well that he surely will *liken* his lover precisely to such a fair object! Second, sometimes rudimentary pairings or comparisons can also have "strength" when the things compared are recognized as strongly opposed to one another. Thus, when Dumont makes comparisons as stark as individualism over

© Equinox Publishing Ltd. 2008

against holism, can there be any doubt that something is afoot—even if we may not know what it is? As some readers may have already detected, Dumont's preferred mode of rudimentary comparison suggests just the opposite of the common tendency of thinking that comparison implies likeness. In fact, Dumont's method is to favor *difference*—a value well lodged in Dumont's moral universe as we have seen. He routinely pits members of a comparison off against each other as *dialectical* opposites. For example, standard in Dumont's comparative logic are oppositions such as pure versus impure in India, Indian "caste" society versus Western "egalitarian" society, French individualism versus German, man-in-the-world versus man-outside-the-world, king versus priest, power versus influence, consanguinity versus affinity, and so on. I think these comparisons can be called "strong" precisely because they are in some way intended to make claims about the *differences* between things, and furthermore, to *make something* of those differences. Notably, Dumont did *not* select Islam for comparison with the West. While the West contrasts sharply with India in being egalitarian and individualist, while India is hierarchical and holist, Islam splits the—dialectical—difference over against the West in being *both* egalitarian, like the West, but holist (anti-individualist) like India. Is the contrast between Islam and the West unimportant in Dumont's mind? No. It is just that it seems not to have been selected, among other things perhaps, because it does not present a *dialectical opposition* with the West.

One can thus see how for Dumont's *comp*aring these things has been an effort at bringing out their differences, not their likenesses. If we are lucky, in the study of religion, for example, we too can debate the hows and whys of the comparison and comparative study of religions, without falling into the naive habit of assuming that those things which we compare are alike. Thus, along with Dumont, we must resist the conventional view that to compare is to "liken," to suggest similarity, analogy, resemblance or equality between those things *compared*. We must liberate ourselves from the notion that "to compare" contrasts to "to contrast" [sic] as in the fusty (and redundant) language of the quiz, test and examination, where we ask students to "compare and contrast" this or that. This usage is redundant, as I think honest reflection and an appreciation of Dumont as a comparativist who emphasizes difference should reveal.

But, of course, when one suggests some serious likeness by pairing things, comparison may court another kind of risk as well. Here, I have in mind certain conventional notions that we unreflectingly entertain in a given culture, or other such notions that social scientists use in *studying* other cultures and societies. It is in this sense that Dumont believes that serious comparison can—and ought—put our fundamental *methodological* categories at risk. Students of culture are not to imagine, therefore,

© Equinox Publishing Ltd. 2008

that they can learn about the others without raising the question of the adequacy of their own categories—about the adequacy of our conventional ways for thinking in the social sciences. The data, so to speak, threaten the observer—an observer who moreover cannot pretend to have a God's eye view of the people one studies. Here, one can imagine that Dumont would have in mind something of what we have already seen in his work on hierarchy and individualism. Regarding individualism, for example, we risk upsetting, or at least changing, our conceptions of who we are by following along with Dumont's arguments in comparing our present-day self-conception with their early Christian groundings, or cross-culturally with parallels to traditional Buddhist and Hindu world renouncers. The single-mindedness and anti-humanistic qualities of the kind of individualism we take for granted may come more sharply into focus by being compared with the anti-social, ascetic severity of the early Christian and Indian parallels.

Social science at risk

How then, in Dumont's mind, do the risks entailed in doing comparison as he proposes particularly threaten professional social scientists? Dumont makes it unmistakably clear that he is unhappy with the way a good deal of his social scientist colleagues carry on with their business, especially when in comes to their employment of cross-cultural comparison. It should come as no surprise then when Dumont rails against the "modern jargon" of the social sciences. His reasons for opposing what he calls "jargon" are not limited, or perhaps even, conditioned by esthetic revulsion. Dumont's wrath is stirred by the analytic inadequacy of which the prevalence of the debased and pretentious language of "jargon" is symptomatic. This

> jargon... provides false assurance and encourages the multiplication of textbooks and increasing specialization; in brief, it supports the vested interests of sociology as a teaching profession, whose function consists essentially in buttressing sociology as a teaching profession.
>
> (Dumont 1975b, 154)

So, Dumont is saying that we need a thorough house-cleaning in the social sciences because of their infection with an ethnocentrism in the form of their culturally-biased conceptual schemes and lexicons. They cannot hope to do defensible comparative work in their present forms because their comparative language is infected with of our modern ideology: our modern social science is "caged within our own frame of reference" (Dumont 1975b, 153). We, therefore, need terms that can accommodate both "us" and "them," and thus *risk* putting our own scientific conceptions of things to the test of their adequacy.

Dumont addresses the question of what one should do about speak-

© Equinox Publishing Ltd. 2008

ing of others comparatively if we abandoned, say, our present culturally-biased "jargon" in the social sciences, by engaging in a little rhetorical jousting. Speaking for his critics, he says. "Then, you will say, what remains of our language if we are asked not to use the categories through which were wont to understand the world?" In effect, Dumont's critics are challenging him by asking him what they will ever do without their culturally-biased "jargon"? To this, Dumont replies, "The answer is simply that we should in the end and on the most general level, rely only on categories that have withstood the fire of comparison" (Dumont 1975b, 156). This language is not easy to create or discover, but we can begin by putting together a comparative lexicon, so to speak, if we keep our wits about us—especially again in regards to deep knowledge of our own modern modes of thinking about them. Indeed,

> each civilization properly conceived should deliver some conclusions of general use, should, that is, provide some elements of a comparative language, some elements that would make the task of comparison easier by degrees. (Dumont 1975b, 159)

Would not it be better for both understanding and for ease of thinking, for example, if we gave up the practice of trying to substitute Western terms like "morality," "duty" and so on for the Indic, "dharma"? Why not start by learning what the far richer term of "dharma" means, and then go on to inform our analyses with it, rather than try to "translate" *dharma* into Western categories that simply never get *dharma* right? Are those in the academic world saying that they are unable to learn new concepts? Are they saying that they are incapable of doing what we do at the popular level all the time? Think about how novel words and concepts like "Zen" have come into the popular vocabulary, even making allowances for the vulgarity of much of the discourse of "Zen." The point is that no one would think of translating "Zen" into its putative Western equivalents. We just learn a new notion, in part, from learning about Japanese Buddhism. So, why cannot our social scientists do as much, Dumont, in effect, is saying? Why not take the *risk* of extending the minds of social science beyond the Western frontier?

In an example of his own choice, Dumont shows what these somewhat abstract words might mean. Here, he appeals to an example from another area of his speciality, South Indian kinship conceptions. Dumont says that most social scientists prefer to speak in terms of the "jargon" of "cross-cousin" marriage for certain preferences in marriage in South India. But, this language fails to give a good account of the "social phenomenon" in question but, argues Dumont, one "more in accordance with the thought of the South Indian people" can (Dumont 1975b, 156). What the language of "cross-cousin marriage" misses is the will of the South Indians to maintain

© Equinox Publishing Ltd. 2008

affinity as a primary kind of relationship, over against, for example, con-sanguinity. For the South Indians it matters more that relations of affinity are expressed, rather than, say, those of consanguinity. For us, Dumont declares, the opposite is true. For us, "affinity is ephemeral." "Blood" is what matters most. Thus, we prefer to conceive of "brother in law"—an affinal relationship—as the consanguineal one of "uncle" to one's son. But in South India, "my mother's brother is essentially my father's brother-in-law,"—an affinal relationship—and, therefore, "his son a kind of in-law to me"—another affinal relationship. He is not my "cousin"—a consanguin-eal relation. Now, in the natural event ("cross-cousin marriage," [sic] so called) when I marry his sister, my mother's brother's daughter, (AKA my "cross-cousin" in our consanguineous system), "I repeat in my generation the same relationship as existed in the previous generation"—"the link that united my father and his brother-in-law is reproduced, or maintained, between their sons, i.e. myself and my 'cousin'" (Dumont 1975b, 156). T.N. Madan, one of Dumont's most devoted critic, sums up Dumont's efforts as showing

> how the so-called cross-cousin marriage is not episodic in character, but actually generates an enduring bond, or 'alliance,' between two patriline-age. This means that in effect a man of a particular lineage *x* shall marry his mother's brother's daughter from lineage *y*, just as his father had done before him, and his son will do after him. (Madan 1999, 476)

Dumont declares this way of seeing things superior because it captures the South Indian commitment to maintaining affinity, especially across generations. We in the West only see affinity synchronically, while the South Indians are determined to insure is diachronically. Standard talk among anthropologists about "cross-cousin" marriage thus utterly misses this central element making up the world view of South Indians. It pro-duces bad "science."

Part of the point here is that the putatively cross-cultural comparative Western social scientific "jargon" of "cross-cousins" simply fails faithfully to represent the priorities of South Indian social reality. It keeps us caged in our own ideology, and never lets us out to meet the other. As such, the standard operating procedure of cross-cultural comparison among most Western social scientists produces an impoverished and finally uninformed account of what is there. On the other hand, Dumont's treatment of mar-riage articulated in terms of ideas like affinity, which are themselves more salient in the Indian context, does much more to help us understand how and why things happen in marriages of so-called "cross-cousins." Adopt-ing the Indian point of view also helps us see the tendencies toward favor-ing relations of consanguinity that are embedded in our own ideologically preferred way of addressing kinship issues. Thus, the process of compari-

© Equinox Publishing Ltd. 2008

son proves to be dialectical—as Dumont argues it should be. Implicitly, he is showing that this knowledge of ourselves gained by encountering the other can produce the special sort of self-knowledge suggested herein. Thus, once we put our Western notions at risk alongside the native Indian categories Dumont's whole approach takes a radical turn: it becomes deliberately self-critical and self-referential, at the same time as it deepens its commitment to the other. Dumont's approach to comparison shows once more that it is a methodology that entails taking *risks*.

Using dialectical opposites to help us think... especially about Western individualism

In emphasizing the elements of challenge and risk, I may perhaps be making too dramatic the entire matter of the operating conditions of cross-cultural comparison. Even if challenges are not delivered or felt by posing items comparatively, one hopes that at the very least comparison makes one think. In this way, comparison may help us encourage an understanding of things by posing them in dialectical relationship to one another. Here, what Dumont hopes to do is not simply "pair up" different things, but pair these different things as dialectical opposites of one another. By now, a well rehearsed example of this would be the way Dumont poses hierarchic or holistic societies over against individualistic ones, caste society over against modern Western society, and so on. The point, however, of posing such things as dialectical opposites is not only to "pair up" opposites, nor even necessarily to issue any challenges, whether subtle or not. But, in pairing up items as dialectical opposites, Dumont believes he can pry out understandings that otherwise would not emerge. In holistic India, for example, Dumont peers into a mirror reflecting an inverted image of the individualist West; when Western individualism is in view, both Indian holism and its traditional form of individualism cast their shadows across Dumont's field of vision. The pattern is dialectical; the projects inseparable. Dumont gets to a deeper understanding of Western individualism by interrogating Hindu holism. And, he believes he can understand *both* better by maintaining them in dialectical comparative relationship with one another. One of his early books, *La Civilisation indienne et nous—Indian Civilization and Ourselves*—subtitled "A *Comparative* Sociological Sketch" conveys this spirit of Dumont's dialectical enterprise (Dumont 1964). Opposites are to be studied together for the sake both of a mutual interrogation and understanding that informs us more than had they been studied individually as autonomous isolates.

What we have already seen of Dumont's program for the study of Western individualist ideology and its relation to "religion," already shows how it emerged from such dialectical projects begun in distant India. Just as

© Equinox Publishing Ltd. 2008

there was something dialectical about Dumont's approach to the relation of individualism to holism, so also can the same be said for his attitudes to India and the West. His career interests have oscillated between East to West over a common ground of hierarchy. In his Indian work, Dumont is well known for his study of Hindu holism, *Homo Hierarchicus* . But he has also worked "the individual's" side of the dialectic, without neglecting the theoretical vision of *Homo Hierarchicus*. In fact, they are internally related. At least since he began publishing expressly on the Hindu "world renouncer" in 1959, this pattern of reciprocal attention seems established (1959). In this landmark essay, "World Renunciation in Indian Religions," Dumont argues that talking about the Hindu individual (world renouncer) requires talking about the world of social relations (caste): "... the secret of Hinduism may be found in the dialogue between the renouncer and the man-in-the-world" (Dumont 1970b, 37). Since the individual, as we know it, and "on the level of life in the world... is not , the only way the individual in India can be conceived is in necessary relation to the world of caste, which the renouncer—by definition—rejects"(Dumont 1970b, 42). Juxtaposition and dialectic then shaped Dumont's use of comparison.

As I have noted in earlier discussions, over the past few years, Dumont has gradually shifted his research interests toward the West. This has left him looking less the sociologist of India and more the intellectual historian of the West—although true to his dialectical or relational style, the change is in ways more apparent than real. For Dumont, this shift actually consists in a movement from the Hindu pole of his unified dialectical comparative concern with India-the West to the Western end of the spectrum. Thus, he remains within the bounds established by the individualism-holism comparative opposition and keeps alive the provocative dialectical tension of seeing this polarity within the comparative context of India and the West. Dialectical opposition once more shapes Dumont's work.

In shifting emphasis from Hindu religion to Western ideology, Dumont has done two things: he has put to one side the traditional holism of caste and its equally traditional renunciation; he has, as we have seen in the previous chapter, applied himself to the problem of the modern emergence of the individual in the West out of its Christian origins and through its early modern developments in economic thought. This has begun a process of "reversing the perspective" of *Homo Hierarchicus*, for the purpose of "throwing light on our modern equalitarian society by contrasting it with the hierarchical society" (Dumont 1977, vii). In 1965, while still writing *Homo Hierarchicus*, Dumont set out on the reciprocal dialectical path of writing intellectual history of the concept of the individual in the West from the vantagepoint afforded by comparative context of the Hindu caste holism (Dumont 1965; Dumont 1982). In dialectic vein again, along with the pub-

© Equinox Publishing Ltd. 2008

lication of *Homo Hierarchicus* in 1966, Dumont wrote a methodological essay exposing the Western individual as an epistemological impediment to sociological comparison with India (Dumont 1970a). Marking the completion of this period of transition from the work of *Homo Hierarchicus* was the aptly named *Homo Aequalis* (Dumont 1977). There, Dumont traced the emergence of the antithesis of Hinduism's renouncer and man in the world of caste, that special breed of Western individualist—*homo economicus.*

In these writings, Dumont has shown how one might go about a comprehensive program of comparative research on Western individualism in dialectical tension with the history of Western ideas and institutions as well as in comparison with Indian holism and world renunciation. But Dumont also shows us more: he shows us how serious engagement in another culture has pushed us to confront the way individualism as our ideology shapes the "others." Conversely, this quest after our own deep assumptions about things requires the standpoint of the "others" to help us make ourselves clear to ourselves. If this dialectic comparative process illuminates our understanding of the individual, perhaps it can do the same for religion, in general?

Comparison sets up a framework for testing hypotheses

The story of the implications of Dumont's promotion of cross-cultural comparison has yet a final chapter. I take it as obvious that in the study of religion, comparison involves much more than the theoretically neutral idea of laying things out in pairs in the way just described—even as this simple operation may at times threaten to put cherished self-images at risk, even as the dialectical opposition of items conduces to creative thinking, even as the perhaps unintentional posing of items in relation to each other may unsettle people, and so on. If one continues with the theme of risk, comparative study of religion as practiced by Dumont shares the view that comparison has higher ambitions even than these we have entertained. Comparison reaches its highest level when it is used to test hypotheses—to raise and answer questions.

We might choose from a number of hypotheses that Dumont tests using comparison. For example, in his study of the rise of Western economic ideology, *Homo Aequalis*, translated unfortunately as *From Mandeville to Marx*, Dumont tells us he seeks to address the question of "how and why his unique development that we call 'modern' occurred at all?" Or, put otherwise, explaining "modern revolution in values represents the central problem in the comparison of societies" (Dumont 1977, 7, 9). In an appendix to *Homo Hierarchicus*, Dumont tests the proposition that modern-day

© Equinox Publishing Ltd. 2008

racism may be a function of the demise of traditional hierarchies (Dumont 1979, Ch. 107). In *Essays on Individualism*, Dumont argues the proposition that totalitarianism might be seen as a "disease" of Western individualism (Dumont 1986a, ch. 6). The same question, now spills out into a torrent series of subsidiary problems, that had been mooted a decade earlier in *From Mandeville to Marx*:

> While political thought... lavishes sophistication on a dead end, the problems that burden the history of the past two centuries are rarely made the object of serious reflection. Are wars and more total and universal wars, dictatorships, and totalitarianism the inevitable accompaniments of modern democracy? Was Tocqueville right in assigning determined conditions and precise limits to the realization of the democratic principle? Or again, has the European workers' internationalist movement been unable to draw the lesson from its reduplicated defeat in 1914 and 1933? Does the marxist socialist theory, to renew or salvage which so much effort is made here and there, belong to the past from that point of view? If so, why? Comparative social science can throw light on those questions which the philosophers neglect. (Dumont 1977, 11)

Dumont's answer is that we have been unable to tackle these questions because we lacked a vantagepoint that would enable us to see our own civilization in a different, more illuminating, light. We need an "external fulcrum" of being able to "see ourselves in perspective" (Dumont 1977, 11). We need a comparative perspective to "see ourselves in perspective" and a strong commitment to comparative methods of explanation.

But, just how does Dumont do this? And, how does the use of comparison help explain solutions to any of these problems? Dumont believes— *hypothesizes*—that we should begin to address such inquiries by taking the position that the West is "exceptional"—that what needs explaining is not "them," but "us" (Dumont 1977, 11)! In logic, if the West is "exceptional," then certain conclusions should follow. For one, Western inworldly individualism is exceptional, and it needs to be explained. We have already seen how Dumont tackles this problem and answers it in our discussion of the rise of individualism in the West in chapter 3. By comparing the origins of individualism in both India and the West, Dumont has argued that the individualists of the West like their Indian "cousins," first, had similar causal bases in movements of out-worldly individualist, world renouncers—in both Christian and Buddhist or Hindu religion. In both cases, individuals could define themselves and their lives over against on-going holistic society, e.g. caste in India or communitarian culture in the West, by appealing to direct contact with, and sanction from the "cardinal element" of the sacred. Early Christians were answerable only to God (Dumont 1985, 94ff). Indian world renouncers bore no allegiance to any political entity.

© Equinox Publishing Ltd. 2008

But, what turned Western individualism toward the "inworldly" Calvinist form that distinguishes our Western individualism from that of our own Western past and both India's past and present? Dumont show that a preparation for Calvinism had been laid down by the Church in a series of increasing engagements by the Church in the governance of the former Roman Empire. With this gradual movement, Christian tradition diverged over the course of centuries from a common scheme found also in India in which a *hierarchical complementarity* was worked out between king and priest. Around 500 CE, Pope Gelasius began a process of the subordination of the king to the priest that stands out starkly against the comparative contrast with India, especially since in the Christian case, the priest asserts priority even in the political realm (Dumont 1985, 107). This movement or departure from the common Hindu and Christian system of *hierarchical complementarity* between political power and religious authority accelerated when, centuries later, the pope added the right to political power to his already full authority in spiritual matters. In comparative contrast again with India's separation of the "two wheels of the dharma," "the divine now claims to rule the world through the Church, and the Church becomes inwordly in a sense it was not heretofore"(Dumont 1985, 111). This papal "power play," if you will, unified the fields of the "mundane" and "spiritual" so that the "Church now pretends to rule, directly or indirectly, the world, which means that the Christian individual is now committed to the world in an unprecedented degree" (Dumont 1985, 113). As such, the Christian individual becomes more "intensely involved in this world"—in effect becomes inworldly—a phenomenon that is not to be seen in the Buddhist world, for example, until the breakdown of the traditional system of separation with the arrival of the notorious "political monks" of South and Southeast Asia (Dumont 1985, 112; Tambiah 1992). So, Dumont, in effect, proves the hypothesis of the exceptionalism of Western individualism by showing how it departed from common Western-Indian origins in the institution of an out-worldly individualism that India still maintains.

Style and substance in Dumont's comparative studies

In conclusion, I have tried to show in this chapter how comparative studies have formed part of both the style and the substance of Dumont's scholarship. He has shown us several different *styles* of comparative method, from the "weaker" heuristic or provocative pairings of one thing against another, to the "stronger" and thus more purposeful dialectical posing of opposites, all the way to Dumont's use of comparison in the "strongest" way possible—to test hypotheses about human religion and culture. I have also strived to argue that Dumont's methodology of comparison— however it is understood along the spectrum from weakness to strength—

© Equinox Publishing Ltd. 2008

is rooted in some core values of Dumont's life. For one, Dumont's orientation to comparison reflects his openness to the "other," and his desire that each and every "other" be open to the reality of each and every opposite "other." This is also to underline Dumont's affection for difference, and his belief that in encountering difference people are made to think. He would, of course, place himself in the first row of those who both have been changed by his encounters with difference, and who embrace it despite the risks entailed. Likewise, his experience with comparison in life and letters, had excited in Dumont a particular delight in challenging both his own culture but more particularly the "culture" of his own profession to be open to the risk that comes from an encounter with difference, and thus with serious work in comparative studies. In my final and concluding chapter, I shall take my departure from these themes of difference and openness to the "other," both in existential and professional senses, by considering the political and moral dimensions of Dumont's thought.

© Equinox Publishing Ltd. 2008

Chapter Five

Conclusion: Dumont's Morality and Social Cosmology

Too liberal for the class from which he came, but not sufficiently enthusiastic for the new ideas envisioned by the republicans, he was adopted neither by the right nor the left. He has remained suspect by all. (Raymond Aron on Tocqueville, Descombes 1999, 84)

I would like to conclude this consideration of the relevance of Louis Dumont's work to the study of religion by giving some attention to the ethical, moral and political questions that have been raised along the way both by this writer and by Dumont's critics.

Readers are by now familiar with the way Dumont argues that our individualist way of thinking produces surprising intellectual "imperialist" consequences. For Dumont, such a disregard for the sensibilities and world views of others amounts to a kind of sin. We arrogantly think that fundamental assumptions about the universality of something as unquestioned as our belief that persons are "individuals" must be true for everyone. On this view, an "individual" is a person endowed with certain "God-given" qualities such as our rights to liberty and equality, and so on. Add to this that such a conception of what it is to be human represents a high point of human development. In the hands of various political or religious powers such assumptions can make huge differences, such as have informed much of the thinking, or so it seems, of the Bush administration and its policies in Iraq. This thinking runs along the familiar lines that since our individualism marks a high point Western cultural, political, religious, esthetic evolution etc., with its emphasis on (the God-given gift of) freedom and such, so also must it be for others. Since our individualism also entails that there be freedom of religion, it also means that religion and political spheres should not interfere with each other—our so-called doctrine of the separation of church and state. In Iraq, then, for example, one might recognize the view held by the "Neo-Conservatives," namely

© Equinox Publishing Ltd. 2008, Unit 6, The Village, 101 Amies Street, London SW11 2JW

that since our Western societies have developed institutions based on individualism, such as parliamentary or liberal democracy or freedom of conscience, and so on, so also others must as well. These assumptions may or may not turn out to be warranted. But, in the short term, they seem to have been mistaken, and tragically so. We imagined that once liberated from Saddam Hussein's tyranny that a Shi'a led majority would soon enough follow the inherent patterns of human political "nature," and give spontaneous birth to the kinds of democratic politics familiar to us in the West. We seem not to have imagined that a Shi'a government might instead look to Islamic models of polity with its suppression of women, for example, that is to say, models of government that tended to look nothing like those that recognized the so-called "God-given gift of freedom." Going further, we seem also to have assumed that civil society in the new Shi'a dominated Iraq would not be dominated by religious law, such as the Muslim *Shari'a*. But, of course, that is precisely what has happened already in parts of the country, and possibly in the future, the entire nation. What Dumont then teaches is that thinking about social cosmology matters— both to avoid the moral offense of ethnocentrism, as well as the real world political consequences such attitudes can have. Nothing much good can come of cultivating *mis*understanding, and that is just what ethnocentrism insures.

Dumont's social cosmology

In my discussion of individualism in chapter 3, I said that Dumont regarded individualism as far more than an ideology applying to the singular human person. As a potentially pervasive ideology, individualism also could structure the way we "construct" or look on the world as a whole. One will recall how Dumont thinks that the situation of Western thinkers, embedded as we are in a world of individualist values and institutions, find it hard to grasp the holism of Indian culture. Indeed, the title of one of Dumont's most important articles reflects this viewpoint—"The Individual as an *Impediment* to Sociological Comparison and Indian History" (my emphasis, Dumont 1970a). Coming as we do from such an individualist civilization, dominated by ideals of liberty, equality and fraternity, we "screen out" whatever does not conform to our expectations, and select instead those features of another culture that do. Consider recent studies of the Protestant Christian biases of early scholars of Buddhism in Sri Lanka that have exposed how these students of Theravada Buddhism made it out to be a kind of "Protestant Buddhism" (Gombrich and Obeyesekere 1988). These Western Buddhologists were simply too eager to see confirmation of the high religious value of their own Protestant religious individualism in both modern-day and historical Theravada. One will recall as well how

© Equinox Publishing Ltd. 2008

in chapter 4, I explored how Dumont's critique of the prevailing conceptualization and category-formation of so-called "cross-cousin marriage" in South India cast actually showed how Western scholars played down holistic and social constructions of this institution in favor of biological ones. Where Dumont saw "affinity" and thus social bonding across generations, those whom he took to task only saw "blood"—consanguinary relationship. While Dumont's appreciation of the impact of individualism on our construction of certain institutions, such as marriage, represents a radical reorientation of methodological thought, he goes further and theorizes about our "*social cosmology*." Dumont offers a theory of both what the basic *species* making up our social world are, as well as how they came into existence. People in the modern West tend to assume that such fundamental categories of our social life, as politics, economics, morality, art, religion, society and so on, are both "natural kinds" and that they name *individual*, distinct and discrete realities. These are the self-contained and autonomous species of socio-cultural life, as much as, at least for long periods of time, under the spell of *Genesis*, the "kingdoms" and "families" of plant and animal life were thought to name *individual* kinds of living things created as such by the Lord High God. Furthermore, some see these individual cultural "kinds" as having the ontological status as substances, that is to say, having some kind of real, as opposed to subjective, *existence*. They are thought to exist objectively. The economy, politics, art, morals, religion and so on are simply *there*; they are simply data, "givens." Thus, the economy has always been with us much as we now understand them. Similarly so has politics and, of course, religion. These individual social species thus are thought to exist independently of human subjectivity, free from our decisions or the vicissitudes of cultural changes that shape our lives.

While many people naively see these objective social species as fixed and unchanging, much as the biblical species of living things are said to be by biblical literalists, they need not be so. They may be seen as the result of great—but objective—processes of change, such as cultural or social evolution. In this way, economics, politics, religion, art and so on are better seen as *relatively* objective and parts of society or culture, products of processes of social change as surely as mountains, rivers and rocks are now seen as products of long-lived and changing processes of natural development. They are no longer to be seen as the eternally fixed, once-and-for-all furniture of our world, but the odds and ends that furnish our social and cultural world at this particular time. As we will see, Dumont will argue that once in the West, we had no "politics," yet lately came to have one. As we have already seen, he takes this historically developmental view about the present-day Western in-worldly individual. At one

© Equinox Publishing Ltd. 2008

time, such a person did not exist in the West, although later, after a long process of historical change, it came to exist.

The moral critique

Dumont upsets scruples among social scientists because he refuses to bring moral considerations to his discussions of "hierarchy." To give "hierarchy" the hearing that Dumont has given it is said by his detractors to be giving an odious moral notion a "platform." It threatens to offend moral convictions and hard-won ethical sensibilities even rigorously and scientifically to entertain what Dumont wants to say. His critics thus, in effect, argue that by Dumont's treating hierarchy as neutral social fact in the spirit of scientific detachment is to violate important moral positions. Would we dignify cliterodectomy in the same way by treating it with the scientific detachment that Dumont proposes? Does this not raise the suspicion that Dumont is indeed trying to promote hierarchy as a real social principle today, and justify it in India in the past and present? Is Dumont's theory of hierarchy truly just a "brahminical" theory, and thus intended to give voice to India's privileged classes over the lower castes (Berreman, 1971, 23)?

Dumont's answer to these charges is rooted in classical anthropological method. Thus, like the French ancestor Montaigne who wrote detachedly about cannibalism, so Dumont takes an open attitude to others. Before any trace of judgment issues from his lips, he seeks understanding from the "natives' point of view," as Geertz has famously said. Dumont believes one ought to try to capture the "totality" of the meanings in human institutions before either praising or condemning them. Beyond that, and betraying again his affinities for the Collége de Sociologie's transgressive ways, puts ourselves and our own way of life at risk. He poses the disturbing question of whether societies based on hierarchy, such as classic India might be revealing things we have chosen to suppress? The "other" may simply be disagreeable because it exposes things we have decided to reject. Are we willing to risk the cultural "comforts" of our own world view? Finally, there is the very real possibility that our ideology may not tell us the whole story about the way things are. Is it not possible that each kind of culture can illuminate something about the general nature of humanity? Do we really think that our society is perfect? Could *any* society be so? Life is perhaps better construed as a balance of trade-offs. Each kind of culture will arrange things so that there are gains and losses. There may be many good values from which to choose, but we must choose to live in one way, and not in another. Dumont is thus advising us to accept what we might call a tragic view of life. We are all winners *and* losers at the same time!

All this implies that some of Dumont's morally concerned critics, such as

© Equinox Publishing Ltd. 2008

At a Glance: The Moral Critique

• Dumont is guilty of promoting immoral social systems such as caste because he refuses to condemn them, and instead seeks to understand them.

• He is himself a crypto-right wing ideologue because he has devoted himself to the explication of what for many in the West is an immoral social system—the caste system.

• But neither of these charges stands up to how Dumont has lived his life. His political affiliations have not been with the right-wing. His commitment to scientific neutrality—even about caste—arises from a profound respect for the "Other" and skepticism about our own moral rectitude.

Gerald Berreman or Rolland Lardinois have just made the first step of their critique a false one (Berreman and Dumont 1962; Lardinois 1996) One may, of course, ask whether Dumont's interrogation of the egalitarian ideal exposes his own right-wing collectivist or conservative positions. But Dumont's actual political alignments speak to another sort of politico-moral configuration. Raymond Aron, Tzvetan Todorov, Luc Ferry, and Bernard-Henri Lévy are more the kin of Dumont than any classic or radical European right-wingers.

Recognizing the "others"

The moral or ethical implications that flow from Dumont's social cosmology are considerable. Straightaway, we can see that Dumont's viewpoint here makes eminent sense when cast against the backdrop of the perennial problem vexing anthropology, namely that of how to avoid ethnocentrism in the study of societies. How does the ethnographer avoid just projecting their own ways of framing and naming reality upon the folk? Dumont's approach to the matter of cross-cousin marriage in South India already should have made it clear that he insists on something like Clifford Geertz's methodological ideal of taking the "native's point of view" into serious consideration—to try to see native institutions as they are understood in the societies into which the anthropologist inquires (Geertz 1983, ch 3).

But, what makes Dumont special is not his insistence upon being sensitive to local issues, like cross-cousin marriage, a particular belief or some such, but his attempts to tackle ethnocentrism at the even more global level of social ontologies. Here, Dumont attacks ethnocentrism at the level of the world organized into its most general domains or cultural catego-

© Equinox Publishing Ltd. 2008

ries, such as art, religion, politics, economy, and so on; or into particular processes producing such domains, such as processes of degeneration and decline or, alternately, evolutionary development and progress. Dumont here serves as a thorough skeptic, and argues the case for cultural difference at a profound level. Do other cultures and societies see the social world as we do? Do they use the same fundamental categories to organize their our social world as we do? We have economics, morality, religion, politics, art and so on. But do they? We assume as natural certain ways of "cutting up the social pie." But, do "they" too separate out their culture into the same *kinds* of "things." In terms of possible parallel processes, since we think of our religious culture as having passed through the historical stages of a gradual evolution from polytheism to monotheism, for example, does that mean that all cultures have done so, or will need to, as well? Unthinkingly so to do may result in what is commonly and rightly condemned as another example of intellectual "imperialism."

The making of Dumont's social cosmology

How did Dumont come to embrace such a *global* vision, when it often seems that the natural tendency of ethnographers is to immerse themselves in the local and never emerge—even as Dumont himself (1986b) urges them so to do! How did Dumont come to think about the great divisions in our ways of thinking about the world? Part of the metaphysical flavor of Dumont's thinking about society in terms of its formal constituent fundamental categories may surely be due to his youthful adventures with the radical intellectuals of the 1930s. In those years, one should recall that it was not only the transgressive thinking of the young Bataille, Caillois, Leiris and others that was all the rage. It was also the rediscovery of Hegel, largely due to the lectures given by Russian emigré, Alexandre Kojéve, that also infused the "air" with grand, if not grandiose, historical theorizing (Kojéve 1988). Dumont's frequent and familiar references to Hegel throughout his work suggest a certain fondness for the kind of thinking one associates with a thinker for whom grand visions were the norm. It was Hegel, said Dumont, who first saw the caste system as a "formal" one that could be reduced to a "structure"—Hegel, said Dumont, "saw the principle of the system in abstract *difference*" (Dumont 1980, 42).

Dumont's philosophical appetites notwithstanding, as he never tires of telling us, he is a devotee of facts and details. This is to say that no matter how philosophical Dumont may range, he remains at heart an anthropologist, even if in the latter part of his career something of an anthropologist of Western ideas. Thus, we need to look for other kindred spirits among Dumont's anthropological associates who might have complemented the Hegelian bent of Dumont's thinking, and especially as that bears on

© Equinox Publishing Ltd. 2008

Dumont's social cosmology. I believe a key person shaping Dumont's view of how one should do anthropology, and thus how we should approach the difficulties of doing justice to the "other," may well have been E.E. Evans-Pritchard. Dumont spent five years in Oxford, lecturing in a department of social anthropology dominated by the great E.E. Evans-Pritchard. His words for his former employer have always been warm. It is, thus, not surprising that in a discussion of one of Evans-Pritchard's better know works, *The Nuer*, that Dumont articulates his global viewpoint about the historicity of our categories, and the consequent need for us to connect with the native point of view and avoid ethnocentrism. In the preface to the French edition of E.E. Evans-Pritchard's classic, *The Nuer*, Dumont argued that Evans-Pritchard and he share the same view as to the ethnocentrism of our Western concept of the political or politics. Dumont, trading on Evans-Pritchard's authority as an ethnographer, takes on the sacrosanct category of the political. Dumont claims that in *The Nuer*, Evans-Pritchard contested the assumption of the universality of the category of "politics." For Dumont the British anthropological Africanist colleagues of Evans-Pritchard simply took as given that since "we have politics, all societies must have them." Representing Evans-Pritchard's contribution to the social epistemology and cultural cosmology, Dumont argued that "there is no guarantee that, just because modern societies clearly distinguish the political dimension, it makes a good comparative dimension" (Dumont 1975a, 337). This led Evans-Pritchard and Dumont to the astounding conclusion that the Nuer seem not to have an autonomous "politics" at all! Instead, they had something like a "system of territorial groups" (Dumont 1975a, 337). There is "order without rule," says Dumont, an "ordered anarchy," citing Evans-Pritchard (Dumont 1975a, 336). But, again astonishingly at least for us in the West, there seems to be no "politics" in our sense.

To better understand this perhaps paradoxical or incredible claim, one should think back to pre-modern Europe where affairs of state were the subject of the life of the court. In the court, there was gossip, scheming and all manner of other goings on. But there was not "politics," in the sense we understand that since the dawning of the modern age with our parliaments, elections, compromises, constitutions, political clubs and parties, and so on. Similarly, totalitarian societies lack a "politics," since the state and its security apparatus make frank and open conversation and assembly impossible. Now just why there is a "politics" in our culture, like the question why there is "economics," "religion," or "art," is partly an historical question. Dumont has argued (1977) that only in relatively recent times in the West have such distinct phenomena emerged (at least putatively) as autonomous phenomena. Moreover, when we speak about

© Equinox Publishing Ltd. 2008

individualism, we are also speaking about the historical emergence of these phenomena: the rise of economics is, in some sense, the same as the rise of economic individualism, the emergence of *homo economicus*. The rise of political individualism—political clubs, parties or associations, the personal values of liberty, equality and fraternity—is likewise a mark of the development of what we call "politics" in the modern sense. In Dumont's view, it was a measure of the greatness of Evans-Pritchard's work that he refused to assume the autonomy of "politics" that came historically, according to Dumont's research, with the advent of individualism. We should not then seek it where it was not to be found—and this against the grain of the prevailing ideology of modern individualism. Says Dumont,

> the pride of place usually granted to politics is due to the reintroduction, whether surreptitious or blatant, but always naive, of the modern individual into a subject where this very book [*The Nuer*] has shown us the opposite path, that of relationship. (1975, 342)

Religion emergent

Just as Evans-Pritchard put the category of the political into question for Dumont, so also did Dumont take on the category of religion. Like his critical discussion of the economic category in *From Mandeville to Marx*, Dumont too has interesting things to say about our concept of religion, especially insofar as it may have an ethnocentric character. While reviewing these debates would carry this discussion too far afield, we might illustrate the nature of these debates by recalling what Durkheim did over one hundred years ago. I believe we can see that Durkheim confronted the prejudices of Western society about the concept of "religion" by challenging the nature of its boundaries. "Religion" was thus not an individual "natural kind" with fixed and eternal conceptual boundaries. It shared cultural space with other putatively individual natural kinds, such as philosophy or morality. This is in effect what Durkheim was doing in challenging the prevailing theistic Western construction of religion as requiring a belief in God or gods. He argued the case that Buddhism ought not be considered just a "philosophy" or "moral system," but ought to be classified as a "religion." This was also to imply that "religion" was not a natural kind distinct from and *individual* with respect to "philosophy" and "morality" to name just two other categories. Durkheim argued that while Buddhism was like a "philosophy" it should nonetheless better be seen as a religion—even though it did not fit the prevailing category definition of religion as requiring a belief in God or gods. Even though not theistic, Buddhism nonetheless should be called a "religion" because it exhibited the same orientation to the "sacred" that theistic religions did. Durkheim in effect tried to broaden

© Equinox Publishing Ltd. 2008

the category, "religion," beyond that current in the West, to include things like Buddhism, which typically were regarded as coming under the rubric of other categories, such as philosophy, morality and so on. Dumont has ventured into the territory of the categorial status of "religion," even if it has not been a major preoccupation. He offers at least part of a theory of the emergence of the category "religion" as a function of our individualist way of constructing the human world. Thus, for Dumont the topic of individualism and religion is not limited to the study of religious individualism, such as evident in movements of freedom of conscience, personal religious devotionalism, and the like. The rise of Protestantism, for instance, does not exhaust the subject of the relation of religion to individualism for Dumont. He wants to argue that the cultural and historical forces embodied in individualism in the West have, in a sense, "made" religion as we know it as the *name of an autonomous* social "kind," fitting alongside economics, politics, art, morality and other members of the bits and pieces that are thought to make up our socio-cultural reality. Dumont comes closest to an explicit statement of his sense of religion's emergence in his Henry Myers Lecture of 1970, "Religion, Politics, and Society in the Individualistic Universe" (Dumont 1971b). This lecture lays down a vision for studying religion in a way that would take into account the present-day individualist theoretical assumptions about the nature of "religion." In part, Dumont undertakes a critique of the category, "religion" that recalls Wilfred Cantwell Smith's attack on the "reified" notion of religion in his *The Meaning and End of Religion* (Smith 1963).

For Dumont, religion figures among the more prominent autonomous realms of politics and economics as a phenomenon connected with the emergence of modern individualism. The ideological specificity of the "religion" of the modern West would have us take it as dealing with otherworldly or so-called spiritual matters, as being distinct from politics, or as something private and interior. For this reason, while religions in this sense have social presences in the West, the rules of our particular "game" dictates that religion is not a form of social organization that competes with the state. It stands over against the state, and can be encompassed by and within the state. It is only with those other conceptions of religion that see themselves as "nations," such as Judaism or as an "*umma*," like Islam that religion and state come into conflict with one another. These other forms of religion threaten to be proverbial "states within the state," a condition intolerable to the modern state, that is to say to our conception of "politics." In nineteenth century America, a similar conflict came necessarily to the fore with the Church of the Latter Day Saints.

Part of what Dumont asserts is that the transition to religion in the modern individualized sense—distinct from politics, economics and such—

© Equinox Publishing Ltd. 2008

entails the abandonment of its once all-embracing character. During the period one might call Christendom, Christianity encompassed and guided economic, political, esthetic and social life. But, ever since the revolutions that made the modern world, Christianity is only a shadow of what it once was as "Christendom." Secularization is nothing else, on Dumont's view, than the division of modern cultural "labor." Social subsystems achieve separation from one another, and maintain no necessary or a priori relations with each other. Today, the trend continues in the West (perhaps especially in Western Europe) such that religion is often reduced to being one individual value system alongside many others. Resistance to this relegation to a value option among many is, of course, at the heart of right-wing Christian unease about the so-called "secular" state. For them, to suggest that religion is an option, is deeply insulting. For them, religion is, rather, an all-encompassing reality that enters and shapes every domain of human life, notably these days, of course, politics and public policy at every level of national life.

An emergent struggle among values: Religion, politics and economics

With the emergence of these newly autonomous subsystems, economics, politics, religion and so on, a kind of struggle for primacy ensues, eventuating in a new order of value. One of the first to attract Dumont's attention was the rise of the modern conception of the individual as a political being. Put otherwise, Dumont showed how the political gradually emancipated itself from the religious and moral, and in effect, how it broke the power of the holistic structures of the medieval Christian system. This individuation of politics from the previously encompassing religious and moral values was achieved in their various ways by both Hobbes and Machiavelli, who together effected a "total break with religion and traditional philosophy." Machiavelli sought to

> disentangle completely political considerations not only from the Christian religion or from any normative model, but even from (private) morality, to emancipate a practical science of politics from all extraneous fetters towards the recognition of its only goal: the *raison d'État*. (Dumont 1986a, 71)

For his part, Hobbes as well excluded "any transcendent norm or value," (Dumont 1986a, 83) as thoroughly as he reduced the social (holism) to the political by making the individual the starting point of the political process, say as an agent in a covenant or contract with other individuals (Dumont 1986a, 85). This is why it is the case in our world, for example, that religion tends to get ranked below, politics and economics, which themselves engage in battles to see which of their priorities shall prevail. One might look, for example, on command economies, also known as socialist societies, as those which have elected that political values will be primary over economic ones. Is there really a demand for so many boots of this or that kind? It matters little, since the political structures of a command society simply order the economic sector to produce such items. In an extreme case, such as in a command economy, political values are supreme and uncontested. All else is subordinated to the power principle. And, this is why Dumont believes that in a society where power sits atop the value hierarchy, especially if it be a false hierarchy, totalitarianism is sure to result. In such a "false" hierarchy, where power is the encompassing value, and if no other values are tolerated, what one gets is an out and out totalitarianism. No other values count. Economics, morality, esthetics: all be damned!

"Real" hierarchy means real tolerance of difference

On the other hand, if the hierarchy be a "true"—Dumontian—one, then power might be the primary value encompassing all others, yet power would recognize other subordinate values as having their place within a common whole making up the "life" of a given society. Here, one does not cleanse the world of all values but one's own. Rather, although one engages in ranking values with respect to one another, the encompassed or opposing values are included as well, at a lower level, in order to complete the whole of which they are part. So, for the sake of the overall health of one's society, one might temper the commands of a given command economy by making allowances for market— economic—considerations. The end result here would be something like the "mixed" economies of the "social democratic" political and economic arrangements that have generally prevailed over the course of the past 60 years or so in Western Europe. Untidy and rife with inconsistencies as these political and economic arrangements are Dumont believes that they, in fact, provide good models of tolerance, and thus of what makes up a viable humane civilization.

In a similar way, Dumont also takes economic society to task. There, the tendency of a society that is embedded in the economy or market is to commodify everything. Making market values the primary and thus encompassing value of a society means that everything has its price, everything is for sale—including every*body* in a strange way. Where the market ascends to the level of an absolute and unquestionable value, such as for certain misnamed "conservative" political parties of the Western world, market solutions are the rule for any problem one might name. Health care? Leave this to the vicissitudes of the market. Environmental issues, such as pollution? The market will magically find an answer to such problems. No "interference" by the political sectors of society are needed or

© Equinox Publishing Ltd. 2008

desired. So, where the market or the economy is left unchecked by "true" hierarchy, commodification can become total. No one who has read Karl Polanyi's *Great Transformation,* and Dumont's lavish praise for this classic of economic history will be surprised by Dumont's horror at the prospects of a society in which everything is for sale, one in which society is embedded in the economy, in short, an unchecked market economy (Dumont 1977; Polanyi 1944). In the West, we may have outlawed slavery and in many places also prostitution or the selling of human body parts, but that does not mean that we have stopped treating persons as things. We still operate on the market basis in so many vital areas of life. Employed at a job, but getting older and more "expensive" in terms of wages or salary? Solution: fire the older—more "expensive,"—worker and hire a younger, "cheaper" one. Treat the working person like a piece of inefficient machinery—a "thing." Modification of this way of treating persons is one achievement of the trade union movement. How then does a Dumontian approach to this well recognized situation take shape? Without denying the claims of market economics that it sits atop the social value system, labor unions negotiate agreements that soften the effects of the market upon individuals. Although society may be "embedded" in the economy, encompassed by the economy, the hierarchy thus established need not be exclusive. It might be an inclusive one that, as Dumont, has elaborated takes in the concerns of the non-primary values. This is, in effect, what labor unions in a mixed economy such as ours does. Not only do unions insist that values opposing the primary economic ones be recognized, but they act through the political structures of society to institutionalize such changes. Legislation tempers the power and influence of the economy and contributes to the conception of a social whole that recognizes values other than the economic. Fair labor practices are put into place, such as forbidding the firing of a worker simply because of their age, and the length of the work day or minimum wage are established. Social security insurance and health care are mandated through the political structures and so on. The result is again a "mixed economy," since social as well as market values are honored for the purpose of the best interests of the whole society. Note however that the hierarchy in which market values encompass the whole remain supreme, and is not essentially overturned; it is only modified so that the encompassed values—the social dimension—has been recognized and given some of its due. Significantly, much of the social legislation mentioned often needs to be justified publically in terms of improving worker efficiency—such as the length of the work week or vacation time so that workers might recuperate from their labor and work even more efficiently upon their return!

The common lesson to be learnt from Dumont's historicizing of the prod-

© Equinox Publishing Ltd. 2008

ucts of the individualist revolution is that we must relativize those very products—especially economics and politics. Dumont is in effect saying that things might be otherwise, and therefore, that assertions of the absolute value primacy of either power or the market can be countered. The present order of things is not "natural," but the product of historical forces and long series of choices. Whatever history should hold for our present dominance by ideas of power and market, Dumont is not prevented from playing the role of social analyst and even prophet when it comes to this new order of things. Dumont, for example, believes that absolutizing either market ideology or power politics has resulted in providing the ideological underpinnings for some of the greatest disasters of the past century. Absolutize power and politics and one gets either Nazism or Stalinism, or both! Absolutize the market and one gets the very conditions that produced forces like Nazism and Communism. After all, they were both radical critiques of economic and political liberalism: market economy inevitably produced depression, chronic unemployment and other economic turmoil that the call for a rigid command economy could not be resisted. Political liberalism, with its fractious party warfare, fed by the pursuit of individual or group self-interest, resulting too often in compromises that pleased no one, cried out as well for the strong hand of a *Führer* or *Il Duce* to silence the "partisan bickering" and to establish national order and progress.

When we come to religion in the modern scheme of things, Dumont presents us with something of a surprise. It is no surprise that modernity ranks religion below secular subsystems, such as politics, economics, and even art. The only condition in which religion could once more rise to the level of primary value and encompass politics, economic and so on would be in some integral nationalism or religious state. This is what Islamicists seek to do in placing their communities under *Shari'a*. It is likewise, some suspect, what the American Christian Right seeks to do in their call for the United States to be recognized as being a so-called "Christian nation." Failing that, religion loses its value with respect to the superior levels. Just as the poor in the world according to Scrooge, religion is left to be eliminated as "surplus population" in hyper-secular modern society. Often this comes in the form of religion being "reduced" to politics or economics. For marxists, economics is the (real) "base" to religion's illusory or ideological "superstructure." As such, religion can only be discussed as epiphenomenal of politics and economics.

Now, none of this is surprising for any student of secularism. What Dumont adds to our understanding can be made clear by some further remarks. While modernity seeks to individualize and thus separate religion from other social entities, as we have seen, religion finds it more difficult to accept this than say economics or politics. The reason for this

© Equinox Publishing Ltd. 2008

is that religion has a "memory," so to speak. It is because religion has had a history of being the one and only encompassing entity that religious folk today find it hard to quite abandon the old status of religion. It is for this reason that integrism seems so easily to reignite its partisans. Unlike politics or economics, Western society was indeed once encompassed in Christian values, and so Christian integrists feel they have special warrant to return the Western world to the way (at least they imagine) it was when religion oversaw and encompassed the entire society. Dumont believes that religion still reflects such "continuity with the traditional universe that remains in the modern universe." Like "society," it reflects the traditional world of holistic values, it can never quite get comfortable with its subordinate role in modern society (1971a, 33).

Tolerance, conflict and recognition: Some moral implications

What summary implications about Dumont's moral vision might we draw from what he has to say about social cosmology? What moral vision lies behind Dumont's readiness to believe ideas about the historical emergence of fundamental social categories in conjunction with arrival of the dominance of the individualist world view in the West? What positive ethical or moral position has Dumont put together in the wake of his explorations into social cosmology and into the subsequent historical analyses that have produced his final works of the sources of Western ideology? I believe these may be listed as an interrelated complex of conviviality, tolerance and recognition of difference.

Consider first what we just have discussed about Dumont's aversion for social value systems that enthrone either power or the market absolutely. This, at the very least, indicates a moderate frame of mind that seeks social arrangement in which violence in itself or violent reaction to dehumanizing social systems is short circuited. Dumont is a peace-maker, and as such a partisan of conviviality. Part of this wish to avoid the conditions that provoke conflict and violence is the secret, I would submit, of Dumont's appreciation of the best of hierarchy. Dumont abhors both totalitarianism and the rule of an unregulated market in part because they will inevitably eventuate in violent conflict. Persons are persons and will not long be treated as things. If their personhood is denied—not recognized—they will use whatever means necessary to force this recognition. Dumont is, accordingly, no libertarian, and certainly no neo-liberal devotee of the so-called "free" market. Neither does he, like the Nietzscheans, such as Foucault, worship at the altar of power (Ferry and Renaut 1997; Strenski 1998). For Dumont, hierarchy teaches a moral vision that seeks conciliation rather than conflict. In this preference for conviviality and peace, Dumont calls familiar allies to his aid—Tocqueville and the sociologist,

© Equinox Publishing Ltd. 2008

Raymond Aron. Dumont tells us that it was Aron who first called his attention to Tocqueville long before Dumont paid homage to Tocqueville in *Homo Hierarchicus*. Aron had argued that Tocqueville had been unjustly crowded out of the upper levels of intellectual discourse by the more fashionable figures of Marx or Nietzsche. Tocqueville had been, in effect, forgotten by the French intellectuals of his generation. Yet Aron believed Tocqueville—especially his *Democracy in America*—deserved serious devotion as one of the "sources of inspiration of sociological thought" (Descombes 1999, 83). In terms of the matters to hand of individualism, hierarchy and conflict, Dumont believed that Tocqueville found the right words to characterize their relationship:

> the individualism that prevails in our societies does not only tend to reserve to the individual a monopoly of meaning. It tends as well to see in conflict the essence of social life and that which binds it together. Now, one cannot say that Tocqueville either denied the importance of conflict, nor that he viewed it as the master or the ultimate motive force in society. On the contrary, for him, conflict is submissive or restrained, that is to say, encompassed. (Descombes 1999, 85)

Tocqueville has, in effect, anticipated Dumont's own formula for hierarchy—the encompassment of the contrary.

If Dumont's debt to Tocqueville is not surprising, his subsequent linking of Tocqueville to the unlikely figure of Hegel surely is—especially since he calls upon Hegel by way of Tocqueville. In a lecture, "Tocqueville et le respect de l'autre," delivered in 1987 on the occasion of his receiving the Tocqueville prize, Dumont concluded with a remarkable assertion, expressed in his most Hegelian—paradoxical and dialectical—style:

> I propose for once to borrow from Hegel—here, from the pre-philosophical Hegel—in order to apply a perfectly hierarchical formula to society by means of which he defined Life. The formula is both dense and difficult to grasp immediately, yet it is at the same time both true and morally sound. Conflict is disunity. But, in society, there is also unity. What is more, disunity is contained in some way in unity. Shall we not then say that according to Tocqueville, society is a unity of unity and disunity?

Typically "dense and difficult" Dumont indeed, but, an adage that should be understandable to those who have followed the exposition of Dumont's ideas in this book. Hierarchy is for Dumont the encompassment of the contrary. Thus, while the principal value of a society is unity, it also embraces disunity, but at a lower level—for the sake, ultimately, of the health and survival of the society as a whole, a unity.

Embracing hierarchy in the interests of social peace casts Dumont in a controversial position that he well appreciates, and endures. Controversially, he believes that while hierarchy, properly understood, works to

© Equinox Publishing Ltd. 2008

overcome conflict, the value that often resists conviviality and generates conflict is equality. Tzvetan Todorov is of the opinion that Dumont "well demonstrated how one is always led to choose between hierarchy or war, and that one can legitimately prefer hierarchy—because ... the principle of equality often generates competition and conflict" (Todorov 2002, 220). Dumont has consistently argued that in conditions where equality and individualism reign untempered by considerations of the whole, instability can prevail. Each individual actor seeks to ensure their equality with each other individual actor. Given that no referee supervises and adjudicates disputes among these actors, they are left to themselves in what can be a Hobbesian war of all against all—a condition of actual or potential conflict. While Dumont prefers a more regulated scheme of things, he realizes that this too has its costs. Dumont believes that no system is perfect and that whatever universe we choose to inhabit, we will unfailingly find that there are "trade offs." Todorov picks up nicely on this aspect of something like a tragic sense of life, common to thinkers like Isaiah Berlin, for example. "Dumont was irritated," says Todorov, "by the ease with which the anti-racist militants of the early 1980s called for 'difference within equality,' but would refuse to take account of the fact that our choices always come at a price. One cannot both have one's cake and eat it too..." (Todorov 2002, 220). In Dumont's mind, "equality" simply means "sameness" among members of the class so designated as "equals." As well meaning as the anti-racist activists may have been, they did not see that their desires ran at cross-currents with themselves. Life is not perfect. Choices need to be made. And, as we discussed in the chapter on hierarchy, as soon as we express a value judgment for something, ipso facto, we subordinate that which we have not chosen. Given the choices involved, we may "hierarchize" that which was not valued; we will include it at a lower level, and encompass it, rather than purging it altogether from our world. But, whatever we do, once we have chosen, we need to pay the "price." So, in this sense hierarchy and conviviality as well have their "price"—as do systems of conflict and equality. Once we choose, we should accept that our choices entail certain consequences.

Taken as positive affirmations, then, Dumont's work points to a second complex of cardinal values that anchors his moral vision—tolerance and recognition of difference. Speaking of Dumont's thought as providing the "tools of tolerance", Vincent Descombes (1999, 78) links tolerance directly, but unconventionally, to the recognition of difference at the heart of Dumont's thinking. Whereas, conventional wisdom might dictate that the key to the recognition of another is recognition of their *equality* with us (recall the experiences of the Dumonts upon first arriving in India), it might actually block recognition of real difference, and thus short-circuit toler-

© Equinox Publishing Ltd. 2008

ance. If the "other" and "we" are "equals," then we are essentially identical. What need then for tolerance? Tolerance only comes into play where difference is real. Tolerance is the hard work of coming to terms with real difference, not ignoring it. Descombes puts it this way: "The recognition of another as an equal is not the recognition of the other *as another*—in its 'difference'—but just the recognition, despite appearances, of the other as not really being different at all" (1999, 81). In our well intentioned desire to link with others, we may actually subsume them to ourselves and our own ideology, and in doing so deny them their voice. What if, as the Dumonts learned to their discomfort in India, the others do not want to be treated as equals?! What if "they" really are different, and insist upon it? In behalf of what virtue would we deny "them" that right? Todorov weighs in as well on this paradox, arguing that Dumont's perspective can help our Western humanists, shaped as they are by the universalist tendencies of the Enlightenment, to overcome even the ethnocentric prejudices embedded in their universalism. If we adopt Dumont's perspective of being open and tolerant of real difference, says Todorov, our humanism will become "tempered by having grasped the heterogeneity of each society, and the differences among societies" (Todorov 2002, 220). Perhaps the creation of this sort of humanism could be said to the highest ethical value to which Dumont and his work aspire?

© Equinox Publishing Ltd. 2008

References

Bellah, R.N., R. Madsen, W.M. Sullivan, A. Swidler and S.M. Tipton. 1985. *Habits of the Heart: Individualism and Commitment in American Life*. Berkeley: University of California Press.

Berlin, I. 1979. The Originality of Machiavelli. In *Against the Current,* ed. I. Berlin, 25–79. London: Penguin.

———. 1990. The Pursuit of the Ideal. In *The Crooked Timber of Humanity,* ed. H. Hardy, 1–19. Princeton, NJ: Princeton University Press.

Berreman, G.D. 1971. The Brahmanical View of Caste. *Contributions to Indian Sociology*, n.s. 16–23.

Berreman, G.D. and L. Dumont. 1962. Discussion of "Caste, Racism and Stratification." *Contributions to Indian Sociology* (n.s.) 6: 122–124.

Bloch, M. 1961. *Feudal Society: The Growth of Ties of Dependence,* trans. L.A. Manyon. Chicago, IL: University of Chicago Press.

———. 1967. A Contribution towards a Comparative History of European Societies. In *Land and Work in Medieval Europe,* ed. M. Bloch, 44–87. New York: Harper.

Bouglé, C. 1899. *Les Idées égalitaires: étude sociologique*. Paris: n/a.

———. 1908 (1927). *Essais sur le régime des castes*. Paris: Alcan.

Bruckner, P. 1992. Le Grand comparateur: un entretien avec Louis Dumont. In *Le Nouvel Observateur*. 2–8 January, 68–70.

Buddharakkhita, V.A.T. (ed.) 1966. *Dhammapada: A Practical Guide to Living*. Bangalore: Buddha Vacana Trust.

Cassian, J. 2000. *The Institutes*, trans. B. Ramsey. New York: The Newman Press.

Celtel, A. 2005. *Categories of the Self: Louis Dumont's Theory of the Individual*. New York: Berghahn Books.

© Equinox Publishing Ltd. 2008, Unit 6, The Village, 101 Amies Street, London SW11 2JW

Chantepie de la Saussaye, P.D. 1897. *Lehrbuch der Religionsgeschichte* 2 vols. Freiburg: np.

Clifford, J. 1988. On Ethnographic Surrealism. In *The Predicament of Culture,* ed. J. Clifford, 117–151. Cambridge, MA: Harvard University.

Collins, S. 1988. *Louis Dumont in the Study of Religions.* Unpublished manuscript.

Delacampagne, C. 1981. Louis Dumont in the Indian Mirror. *RAIN* 43: 4–7.

——. 1984. Louis Dumont. In *Entretiens avec Le Monde,* ed. anon. Paris: La Découverte/Le Monde.

Descombes, V. 1999. Louis Dumont ou les outils de la tolérance. *Esprit* 252: 65–85.

Dumont, L. (ed.) 1970. *Religion/ Politics and History of India.* Paris: Mouton.

——.1951. *La Tarasque: essai de description d'un fait local point de vue ethnographique.* Paris: Gallimard.

——. 1959. Le renoncement dans les religions de l'Inde. *Archives de sociologie des religions* 4: 45–69.

——. 1964. *La Civilization indienne et nous.* Paris: Armand Colin.

——. 1965. The Modem Conception of the Individual: Notes on Its Genesis. *Contributions to Indian Sociology* (n.s.) 8: 13–61.

——. 1970a. The Individual as an Impediment to Sociological Comparison and Indian History. In *Religion/Politics and History of India,* ed. L. Dumont, 133–151. Paris: Mouton.

——. 1970b. World Renunciation in Indian Religions. In *Religion/Politics and History in India,* ed. L. Dumont, 33–61. Paris: Mouton.

——. 1971a. On Putative Hierarchy. *Contributions to Indian Sociology (n.s.)* 5: 61–81.

——. 1971b. Religion, Politics, and Society in the Individualistic Universe. *Proceedings of the Royal Anthropological Institute for I970.* 1971: 31–41.

——. 1975a. "Preface" by Louis Dumont to the French Edition of *The Nuer.* In *Studies in Social Anthropology,* eds. J. Beattle and R.G. Lienhardt, 328–342. Oxford: Oxford University Press.

——. 1975b. On the Comparative Understanding of Non-Modern Civilizations. *Daedalus* 104: 153–172.

——. 1977. *From Mandeville to Marx: The Genesis and Triumph of Economic Ideology.* Chicago, IL: University of Chicago Press.

——. 1979a. The Anthropological Community and Ideology. *Social Sciences Information* 18: 785–817.

© Equinox Publishing Ltd. 2008

———. 1980. *Homo Hierarchicus,* trans. L.D. Mark Sainsbury, Basia Gulati. Chicago, IL: University of Chicago Press.

———. 1981. Les origines chrétiennes de l'individualisme moderne. *Le Débat* 15: 124–146.

———. 1982. A Modified View of Our Origins: The Christian Beginnings of Modern Individualism. *Religion* 12: 1–27.

———. 1983. *Essais sur l'individualisme: une perspective anthropologique sur l'idéologie moderne.* Paris: Seuil.

———. 1985. A Modified View of Our Origins: the Christian Beginnings of Modern Individualism. In *The Category of the Person: Anthropology, Philosophy, History,* eds. M. Carrithers, S. Collins and S. Lukes, 93–122. Cambridge: Cambridge University Press.

———. 1986. On Value. In *Essays on Individualism: Modern Ideology in Anthropological Perspective,* ed. L. Dumont, 234–268. Chicago, IL: University of Chicago Press.

———. 1986a. *Essays on Individualism: Modern Ideology in Anthropological Perspective.* Chicago, IL: University of Chicago.

———. 1986b. Genesis, I: The Christian Beginnings: From the Out worldly Individual to the Individual-in-the-World. In *Essays on Individualism: Modern Ideology in Anthropological Perspective,* ed. L. Dumont, 23–59. Chicago, IL: University of Chicago Press.

———. 1986c. Marcel Mauss: A Science in Becoming. In *Essays on Individualism,* 183–200. Chicago, IL: University of Chicago Press.

———. 1994. *German Ideology: From France to Germany and Back.* Chicago, IL: University of Chicago Press.

Durkheim, É. 1975. Individualism and the Intellectuals. In *Durkheim on Religion,* ed. W.S.F. Pickering, 59–73. London: Routledge.

———. 1982. *The Rules of Sociological Method and Selected Texts on Sociology and its Method* (trans.) W.D. Halls. London: Macmillan.

Evans-Pritchard, E.E. 1962. Religion and the Anthropologists. In *Essays in Social Anthropology,* ed. E.E. Evans-Pritchard, 29–45. London: Faber and Faber.

———. 1981. *A History of Anthropological Thought.* New York City: Basic Books.

Ferry, L. and A. Renaut. 1990. *French Philosophy in the Sixties: An Essay on Antihumanism,* trans. M.S. Cattani. Amherst: University of Massachusetts.

Ferry, L. and A. Renaut (eds) 1997. *Why We Are Not Nietzscheans.* Chicago, IL: University of Chicago.

© Equinox Publishing Ltd. 2008

Galey, J.-C. 1982. A Conversation with Louis Dumont, 12 December 1979. In *Way of Life: King, Householder, Renouncer. Essays in Honour of Louis Dumont,* ed. T.N. Madan, 13–22. Paris: Editions de la Maison des Sciences de L'Homme.

Geertz, C. 1983. *Local Knowledge: Further Essays in Interpretive Anthropology.* New York: Harper and Row.

Godelier, M. 1999. *The Enigma of the Gift,* trans. N. Scott. Chicago, IL: University of Chicago.

Gombrich, R. and G. Obeyesekere. 1988. *Buddhism Transformed: Religious Change in Sri Lanka.* Princeton. NJ: Princeton University Press.

Haidt, J. 2007. The Spirit of Dharmacracy. In *Los Angeles Times.* Los Angeles. 14 January, M3.

Heft, J.L. (ed.) 1999. *A Catholic Modernity? Charles Taylor's Marianist Lecture.* New York: Oxford University Press.

Hubert, H. 1904. Introduction — la traduction française. In *Pierre Daniel Chantepie de la Saussaye, Manuel de l'histoire des religions,* eds. H. Hubert and I. Lévy, v–xlviii. Paris: Colin.

Jones, R.A. 1977. On Understanding a Sociological Classic. *American Journal of Sociology* 83: 279–319.

Karady, V. (ed.) 1974. *Marcel Mauss: Oeuvres 2. Représentations collectives et diversité des civilisations.* Paris: Minuit.

Khare, R.S. (ed.) 2006. *Caste, Hierarchy and Individualism: Indian Critiques of Louis Dumont's Contributions.* New Delhi: Oxford University Press.

Köbben, A.J.F. 1970. Comparativists and Non-Comparativists in Anthropology. In *A Handbook of Method in Cultural Anthropology* (eds) R. Narroll & R. Cohen. New York City: Columbia University Press.

Kojéve, A. 1988. Hegelian Concepts: Saturday, December 4, 1937. In *The College of Sociology, 1937–39,* ed. D. Hollier, 85–93. Minneapolis: University of Minnesota Press.

Kolenda, P. 1976. Seven Kinds of Hierarchy in *Homo Hierarchicus. Journal of Asian Studies* 35: 581–596.

Lardinois, R. 1996. The Genesis of Louis Dumont's Anthropology: The 1930's in France Revisited. *Comparative Studies of South Asia, Africa and the Middle East* 16: 27–40.

Lévi-Strauss, C. 1963. Totemism (trans.) R. Needham. Boston: Beacon.

———. 1967. *The Scope of Anthropology.* London: Jonathan Cape.

———. 1987. *Introduction to the Work of Marcel Mauss.* London: Routledge.

© Equinox Publishing Ltd. 2008

Lilla, M. 1999. Necrology: Louis Dumont. *Correspondence.* Spring-Summer 4, 41.

Lukes, S. 1972. *Emile Durkheim.* New York: Harper and Row.

Macfarlane, A. 1978. *The Origins of English Individualism.* Cambridge: Cambridge University Press.

Madan, T.N. 1999. Louis Dumont 1911–1998: A Memoir. *Contributions to Indian Sociology* (n.s.) 33: 473–501.

Marriott, M. 1966. The Feast of Love. In *Krishna: Myths, Rites, and Attitudes,* ed. M. Singer, 200–212. Chicago, IL: The University of Chicago Press.

Parkin, R. 2003. *Louis Dumont and Hierarchical Opposition.* New York: Berghahn Books.

Polanyi, K. 1944. *The Great Transformation.* New York: Farrar and Rinehart.

Radcliffe-Brown, A.R. 1958. *Method in Social Anthropology.* Chicago, IL: University of Chicago Press.

Sangharakshita, B.S. 1995. *The Inconceivable Emancipation: Themes from the Vimalakirti-Nirdesa.* Cambridge: Windhorse Publications.

Sen, A. 2005. *The Argumentative Indian: Writings on Indian History, Culture and Identity.* New York: Farrar, Straus and Giroux.

Shanahan, D. 1992. *Toward a Genealogy of Individualism.* Amherst: University of Massachusetts Press.

Singer, M. 1972. Industrial Leadership, the Hindu Ethic, and the Spirit of Socialism. In *When a Great Tradition Modernizes,* ed. M. Singer, 272–366. London: Pall Mall Press.

Smelser, N. 1976. *Comparative Methods in the Social Sciences.* Englewood Cliffs: Prentice-Hall.

Smith, W.C. 1963. *The Meaning and End of Religion.* Minneapolis: University of Minnesota Press.

Spiro, M.E. 1970. *Buddhism and Society.* New York: Harper and Row.

Stocking, G.W. 1987. *Victorian Anthropology.* New York: Free Press.

Strenski, I. 1985. What Structural Mythology Owes to Henri Hubert. *Journal of the History of the Behavioral Sciences* 21: 354–371.

———. 1998. Religion, Power and the Final Foucault. *Journal of the American Academy of Religion* 66(2): 345–368.

———. 2005. Engaging the Believer. *Religion and Education.* 32(1): 42–45.

Tambiah, S.J. 1992. *Buddhism Betrayed: Religion, Politics and Violence in Sri Lanka.* Chicago, IL: University of Chicago Press.

© Equinox Publishing Ltd. 2008

Todorov, T. 1999. *The Conquest of America: The Question of the Other*, trans. R. Howard. Norman: University of Oklahoma Press.

———. 2002. *Devoirs et délices: une vie de passeur. Entretiens avec Catherine Portevin*. Paris: Seuil.

Ward, B. 2003. *The Desert Fathers: Sayings of the Early Christian Monks*. London: Penguin.

Watt, I. 1996. *Myths of Modern Individualism: Faust, Don Quixote, Don Juan, Robinson Crusoe*. Cambridge: Cambridge University Press.

© Equinox Publishing Ltd. 2008

Index

A

affinity, in kinship, 108, 111, 121
Althusser, Louis, 9
Annales School, 6, 16, 97, 98, 100
anthropology:
  caste and, 3, 23
  comparative method and, 89, 91
  religion and, 1, 16
  See also caste; Clifford, James;
    Douglas, Mary; Evans-Pritchard,
    E.E.; Geerz, Clifford; India; kin-
    ship; social science
anti-modernism, 9, 22, 31
Aquinas, Thomas, 73
Aron, Raymond, 9, 28, 119, 123, 133
artha, 62, 65, 70
ātman, 63

B

Barth, Karl, 107
baseball, 102
Bataille, Georges, 7, 30, 32, 124
Benedict XVI (Pope), 107
Berlin, Isaiah, 25, 41, 46–48, 134
Berreman, Gerald, 3, 27, 51, 123
Bhagavad Gita, 72
*bhikkhu*s, 55, 64, 69, 72
Bible, 62, 78, 79, 121
Bloch, Marc, 16, 22, 94, 95, 97, 98, 99
Bouglé, Célestin, 12, 13
Brāhmin ("holy power"), 63–64
Brāhmins (caste), 10, 39, 40, 60, 61,
  62–63, 66–67
  See also caste
Braudel, Ferdinand, 6

Buddhism:

*bhikku*s, 55, 64, 69, 72
Buddha, the, 62
caste and, 44, 61, 62
Dhammapāda, 66, 67, 68
Hinduism and, 44–46, 47, 48
politics and, 116
as religion, 126–127
scholars of, 126
self and, 64
values of, 44–46, 47, 48
world-renouncing and, 66, 67–68,
  69, 115
Zen and, 110
See also dharma

C

Caillois, Roger, 5, 7, 9, 30, 124
Calvinism, 71, 72, 81, 116
Cassian, John, 78, 83
caste (*jāti*):
  Dumont's attitude to, 2, 31, 33, 51
  Dumont's works on, 6, 18, 36
  as Durkheimian interest, 13, 44
  Hegel and, 124
  hierarchy and, 3, 4, 8, 12
  Holī and, 40
  individualism and, 27, 28, 55, 57, 71
  trade guilds and, 74
  world-renouncing and, 55–56, 60–62,
    64–67, 113
  See also Brāhmins; hierarchy;
    holism; *Homo Hierarchicus;*
    Kṣatriyas; Śūdras; Vaiśyas; Un-

© Equinox Publishing Ltd. 2008, Unit 6, The Village, 101 Amies Street, London SW11 2JW

touchables
Centre d'Études indienne, 6
Chantepie de la Saussaye, Pierre
    Daniel, 106, 107
Christianity:
  Aquinas, Thomas, 73
  Benedict XVI (Pope), 107
  Calvinism, 71, 72, 81, 116
  capitalism and, 65
  Christendom and, 86, 128
  Christian Right, 86, 131–132
  "culture war" and, 70
  Desert Fathers, 79–80, 83
  equality and, 71–72
  Gelasius (Pope), 81, 116
  hierarchy and, 21–22, 34
  individualism and, 20, 57, 59, 71–72,
      77–80, 116, 127
  inworldliness and, 81–82
  Jesus Christ, 78, 79, 96
  Luther, Martin, 71
  Mediterranean, 101
  morality and, 25, 46–47
  "paganism" and, 96–97
  Paul, St., 78, 79
  Puritanism and, 75
  study of Buddhism and, 126
  See also Bible; monasticism; secu-
      larization; inworldliness
Church of the Latter Day Saints, 127
Civilisation indienne et nous (Dumont),
    6, 18, 112
Clifford, James, 29–30
cliterodectomy, 23, 122
Collège de Sociologie, 5, 7, 29, 30, 32,
    44, 122
Collins, Steven, 7, 10
commodification, 129–130
Communism, 41, 131
  See also Marx, Karl; Stalin, Josef
community, 4
  See also hierarchy; individualism
comparative method:
  dialectic and, 108, 112–114, 116

difference and, 103–104
Durkheim and, 97–99
Guénon and, 10–11
kinship and, 111
India and the West and, 57–58
language and, 110–111
political thought and, 115
religion and, 89, 90, 93, 95–97, 105,
    106–107
risk and, 104–106, 107, 112
"strong", 90–92, 94–98, 101, 106,
    107–108, 116–117
Tarasque and, 99–101
"weak", 92–93, 116–117
See also comparison, cross-cultural
comparison, cross-cultural:
  India and China, 9
  India and the West, 17–19, 53, 54,
      57–58, 108, 112–114, 115
  Islam and the West, 108
  See also comparative method; hier-
      archy; holism; individualism
consanguinity, 108, 111, 121
Contributions to Indian Sociology (jour-
    nal), 6, 18, 73
cricket, 102–103
"cross-cousin marriage", 110–111, 123

D

Declaration of the Rights of Man and
    Citizen, 73
Delacampagne, Christian, 23
Democracy in America (Tocqueville), 53
Descombes, Vincent, 134–135
Desert Fathers, 79–80, 83
Dhammapāda, 66, 67, 68
dharma:
  caste and, 62
  as duty, 65, 110
  transcendence of, 66–68, 69, 70
  "two wheels of", 116
dialectic, 108, 112–114, 116
  See also comparative method
difference, 103–104, 108, 117, 124,

© Equinox Publishing Ltd. 2008

134–135
See also comparative method
Douglas, Mary, 6
Dreyfus Affair, 51–52, 86
Dumézil, Georges, 5, 100
Durkheim, Émile:
　on Buddhism, 126
　comparative method and, 89, 91, 95,
　　97–99
　Dumont and, 14, 16, 43–44, 97, 105
　Durkheimians, 6, 12, 13, 16
　individualism and, 51–52, 59, 86
　influence of, 16
　Lévi-Strauss and, 1
　Mauss and, 29

E

École des Hautes Études en Sciences
　Sociales, 1, 6, 16, 18
École Polytechnique, 5
École Pratique des Hautes Etudes, 6,
　15, 16, 18
economics:
　equality and, 41–42
　as ideology, 2, 121, 124, 125–6, 127,
　　128–132
　individualism and, 74, 75, 84, 85, 114
egalitarianism:
　Christian, 78
　conflict and, 134
　fairness and, 10, 49
　hierarchy and, 22, 33, 108
　liberty and, 9–10, 41, 52
　queried, 2, 27
　religious, 71–72
　valuation and, 36–37
　Western, 73–74
　See also individualism
egotism, 26, 53, 55
Egypt, 95–96
empathy, 31
encompassment of the contrary,
　38–40, 41, 43, 48
Enlightenment, the, 4, 73, 76, 104, 135

equality. *See* egalitarianism
Essai sur le régime des castes
　(Bouglé) 12, 13
Essais sur l'individualisme (Dumont) 6,
　17, 19, 57, 77, 115
ethnocentrism, 109, 120, 123–125, 135
　See also comparative method
Evans-Pritchard, E. E., 6, 16, 83–84,
　91, 94, 125–126
evolutionary schemes, 94, 95, 124

F

"fable of the bees", 75
fascism. *See* totalitarianism
Febvre, Lucien, 16
Ferry, Luc, 9, 28, 123
Feyerabend, Paul, 11
Finkielkraut, Alain, 9
Foucault, Michel, 132
France:
　Dreyfus Affair, 51–52, 86
　Frankish Kingdom, 82
　French Revolution, 52–53
　individualism and, 86
　intellectuals, 3, 9–10, 52
Frazer, James, 91, 94, 96–97, 99
French Revolution, 52–53, 73–74
From Mandeville to Marx (Dumont).
　See Homo Aequalis I

G

Geertz, Clifford, 123
Gelasius (Pope), 81, 116
gender relations, 79
German Ideology (Dumont). *See
　Homo Aequalis II*
Godelier, Maurice, 1
Guénon, René, 7–9, 10–13, 14, 29,
　30, 31

H

Haidt, Jonathan, 41, 44
hands, left and right, 26, 33–35, 36–37,
　38–39, 40, 42, 43

© Equinox Publishing Ld. 2008

Hegel, G.W.F., 124, 133
hierarchy:
  advantages of, 28–29
  complementarity and, 38, 62, 70,
    81–82, 116
  defined, 26, 31–36
  encompassing the contrary and,
    38–39, 41, 42, 46, 48, 81–82, 133
  evaluation and, 41–43
  holism as, 24, 25, 26, 36, 43–44
  as ideology, 25–26
  impediment to understanding, 25
  individualism as, 24, 27, 59, 86
  inequality and, 36–37, 39, 49
  legitimacy of, 22–23, 27, 122
  as opposite of individualism, 3–4,
    17–19, 53, 54, 58, 112
  oppositions and, 26, 33–34, 35, 36–38
  power relations and, 33–34
  reversal and, 39–40
  sacred, 21–22
  tolerance and, 70, 129
  totalitarianism and, 129
  as transgressive idea, 5, 20, 30–31, 35
  See also caste; hands, left and right;
    holism; *Homo Hierarchicus*;
    individualism
Hinduism:
  artha, 62, 65, 70
  ātman, 63
  Buddhism and, 44–46, 47, 48, 66
  commodification and, 130
  conciliation and, 132, 133–134
  difference and, 48–49
  Guénon and, 7–8
  Holī, 40
  Krishna, 40, 72
  mokṣa, 65, 68, 70
  purity and, 39, 63, 66–67, 108
  sannyāsīns and, 55, 61
  See also caste; *dharma*; holism;
    India; man-outside-the-world;
    world-renouncing
Hobbes, Thomas, 74, 128, 134

Holī, 40
holism:
  in Dumont's work, 17
  as hierarchy, 24, 25, 26, 36, 43–44
  and individualism, 59, 60, 112
  See also hierarchy
*Homo Aequalis I: genèse et
  épanouissement de l'idéologie
  économique (From Mandeville to
  Marx, Dumont):*
  and economics, 114, 126
  and *Homo Hierarchicus*, 57–58
  and politics, 115
  publication of, 6, 17
*Homo Aequalis II: L'idéologie al-
  lemande: France–Allemagne et
  retour (German Ideology: From
  France to Germany and back,
  Dumont), 6–7, 17, 19, 57–58, 99*
Homo Hierarchicus (Dumont):
  critical reaction to, 3, 29, 31, 32, 51
  Durkheim and, 44
  place in Dumont's work, 2, 15, 17,
    18, 36, 56, 57, 113–115
  Tocqueville and, 133
  See also caste, hierarchy
human rights, 80
humanism, 135

I

Idées Égalitaires: étude sociologique
  (Bouglé), 13
ideology:
  hierarchy as, 25–26
  individualism as, 19
  religion and, 20
  social science and, 109, 122
India:
  China and, 9
  field research in, 5–6, 15, 18, 56,
    103–104, 135
  as opposite to West, 17–19, 53, 54,
    57–58, 108, 112–114, 115
  See also caste; hierarchy; Hinduism;
    kinship

© Equinox Publishing Ltd. 2008

"Individual as an Impediment to Sociological Comparison and Indian History" (Dumont), 57, 120
individual, the, 54, 59, 113–114,
121–122
See also individualism
individual-outside-the-world. *See* man-
outside-the-world
individualism:
caste and, 56–57, 71
Christian origins and, 20, 57, 59,
76–80, 116
comparative method and, 109
conflict and, 133–134
defined, 58–59
dharma and, 65, 66–67
disadvantages over hierarchy, 28–29
Dumont's works on, 6–7
as hierarchy, 24, 27, 59, 86
as ideology, 18, 20, 54–55, 59, 114
as impediment to understanding
hierarchy, 25
liberty and, 41–42, 45, 119–120
as opposite of hierarchy, 3–4, 17–19,
53, 54, 58, 112
modern, 80–82
political and economic, 84, 128–129
religion and, 85–87, 127–128
self and, 63–64
social explanations and, 43
value of, 51–54
Western, 71–75, 84, 113–114, 119–120,
133
See also hands, left and right; hierarchy; individual, the; inworldliness;
world-renouncing
"influence", intellectual, 11–12
Institut d'Ethnologie (Paris), 5
Institute of Anthropology (Oxford), 6, 18
*Introduction générale è l'étude des
doctrines hindouse* (Guénon), 7
inworldliness, 71–72, 82, 83, 115, 116,
121–122
See also individualism; man-in-the
world; world-renouncing

Iraq, US invasion of, 119–120
Islam:
in Iraq, 120
Shari'a, 129, 131
Shi'a, 120
state and, 86, 127, 131
Sufism, 7, 8
veiling, 79
West and, 108

J

Jainism, 61, 62
jargon, 109–111
jāti. See caste
Jesus Christ, 78, 79, 96
See also Christianity
Jones, Robert Alun, 12
Judaism, 127

K

kāma, 62, 65, 70
kinship:
affinity and consanguinity, 108, 111,
121
"cross-cousin marriage", 110–111
structuralism and, 15
world-renouncing and, 60, 65, 67–68
Kojéve, Alexandre, 124
Kolenda, Pauline, 32
Krishna, 40, 72
Kṣatriya, 10, 60, 62, 63

L

language:
comparative study of, 89, 102
Dumont's study of, 14, 56
jargon, 109–111
Lardinois, Rolland, 7–9, 10–12, 27,
30, 123
las Casas, Fra Bartolomé de, 24
Leenhardt, Maurice, 1, 15
Lévi, Sylvain, 2, 13
Lévi-Strauss, Claude:
binary oppositions and, 38
Dumont and, 5, 9, 13, 15

© Equinox Publishing Ld. 2008

Mauss and, 14
religion and, 1–2
Lévy, Bernard-Henri, 28, 123
liberty, 41
Lilla, Mark, 1, 52
lord of misrule, 39
Luther, Martin, 71

M

Machiavelli, Nicolo, 25, 46–47, 74, 86, 128
Madan, T.D., 74–75, 111
Man and His Becoming according to the Vedanta (Dumont), 7
man-in-the-world, 56, 64–65, 69–70, 77, 108, 113
  See also inworldliness; man-outside-the-world; world-renouncing
man-outside-the-world, 60, 64–65, 69–70, 108
  See also inworldliness; man-in-the-world; world-renouncing
Mandeville, Bernard, 75
Maoism, 9
market values, 129–131, 132
Marriott, McKim, 43–44
Marx, Karl, 10, 43, 133
  Marxism, 9, 86, 115, 131
  See also Communism
Mauss, Marcel, 5, 7, 8, 9, 12–15, 18, 29–30, 97
Mayakovsky, Vladimir, 93
medievalism, 22, 34, 40
Meillet, Antoine, 97, 98
Mexico, 94–95
modernity, and individualism, 74–75
"Modified View of Our Origins" ("Les origines chrétiennes de l'individualisme moderne", Dumont), 19, 57, 75–77
mokṣa, 65, 68, 70
monasticism:
  Buddhist, 44–45, 55
  early Christian, 79–80, 83

Western, 54, 55, 70, 72
  See also world-renouncing
Montaigne, Michel de, 122
morality
  Christianity and, 25, 46–47
  judgements in research, 122–123
  as part of social realm 124
  Roman 46–47
  and world-renouncing, 67–68
  See also caste; cliterodectomy; egalitarianism; hierarchy; pluralism, of values
Musée National des Arts et Traditions Populaires, 5, 13, 14–15, 16, 100
Müller, Max, 89

N

nationalism, 77
Nazism, 28, 131
  See also totalitarianism
Neo-Conservativism, 119
Nuer, the, 83–84, 125–126
New Testament, 78, 79
Nibbāna, 64
Nietzsche, Friedrich, 28, 133
  Nietzscheans, 132

O

oppositions:
  emcompassed, 38–40, 41, 43, 48
  hierarchy and, 26, 33–34, 35, 36–38, 40
  See also pluralism, of values
"origines chrétiennes de l'individualisme moderne" (Dumont).
  See "Modified View of Our Origins"
Other, the, 23–24, 58, 103, 114, 117, 123–125, 135
out-worldliness. *See* world-renouncing

P

"paganism", and Christian origins, 96
Pali Canon, 64, 67, 68, 69

© Equinox Publishing Ltd. 2008

Parkin, Robert, 28, 51, 99
Parson's Law, 101
Paul, St., 78, 79
Paulhan, Jean, 11, 100
Phoney War (Drole de Guerre), 5, 14
Pippin (King of the Franks), 82
Place de la Concorde, human sacrifice in
pluralism, of values, 25, 41, 46, 47
    See also morality; oppositions
Pocock, David, 6, 18
Polanyi, Karl, 130
politics:
    as category, 2, 121, 124, 125–126,
        127, 131–132
    Dumont's, 8, 9–10, 28, 119
    hierarchy and, 129, 131
    religion and, 75, 127, 128, 131
    See also Communism; Nazism;
        socialism; Stalin, Joseph; totalitari-
        anism
pollution, 67
    See also purity, in Hinduism
power, as encompassing value, 129,
    131, 132
Pramalai Kallar, 5
purity, in Hinduism, 39, 63, 66–67, 108

R

racism, 2, 3, 115
    anti-racists, 134
Radcliffe-Brown, A.R., 6, 16, 89
Reformation, the, 4, 71–72
religion, study of:
    anthropology and, 1, 16
    Buddhism and, 110, 126
    comparative method and, 89, 90, 93,
        95–97, 105, 107, 108–109
    in Dumont's work, 76–77, 87
    hierarchy and, 44
    individualism and, 85, 119
    religion as category and, 126–128
    scholars of, 2
    study of ideology and, 20
Religion/Politics and History in India
    (Dumont), 6, 17

"Religion, Politics, and Society in the
    Individualistic Universe" (Dumont),
    84–85, 127
Renou, Louis, 15
renouncers. *See* world-renouncing
Rivière, Georges-Henri, 5, 100, 101
Roman Empire, morality of, 46–47

S

sacred:
    Bataille and, 32
    Durkheimian, 1
    hierarchy and, 21
sacrifice, 63, 65, 67
    human, 30, 32, 95–96
salvation, in Hinduism, 63
*sannyāsīn*s, 55, 60–63, 66, 67, 69, 72
    See also Hinduism; world-renouncing
Sanskrit, 5, 14
Sartre, Jean-Paul, 9
Savonorola, 25
Schubring, Walther, 5, 14, 18
science, 11, 98
    See also social science
secularization, 85–86, 128, 131–132
Sen, Amartya, 61
Shakespeare, William, 107
Singer, Milton, 72
Smart, Ninian, 96
Smith, Adam, 43, 75
Smith, William Cantwell, 85, 127
social cosmology, 121, 132
social ontologies, 83, 123–124
social science, 109–111, 122
    See also anthropology
socialism, 129
    See also Marx, Karl
Sous-caste de l'Inde du Sud (Dumont),
    6, 18
Spiro, Melford, 66
Stalin, Josef, 92–93
    Stalinism, 10, 27, 52, 57, 131
    See also totalitarianism
structuralism, 1, 14, 15, 17

© Equinox Publishing Ld. 2008

See also Lévi-Strauss, Claude
Śūdra, 60, 62, 63
Sufism, 7, 8
  See also Islam
surrealism, 30
Syncletia, St., 80

T

Tamilnadu, 6
Tarascon (Provence), 5, 11, 15, 100–101
Tarasque (Dumont)
  and comparative method, 99–101
  in Dumont's works, 5
  and material culture 16, 98
  and Mauss, 14, 15
  publication, 11, 18
Taylor, Charles, 80
Tocqueville, Alexis de, 52–53, 115, 119,
  132–133
Todorov, Tzvetan, 1, 9, 10, 24, 28, 123,
  134, 135
tolerance, 70, 129, 134–135
totalitarianism, 2, 27–28, 129
transgression, 30–31, 35, 44, 122
trust, 44
Turkey, 4–5, 7
Tylor, Edward Burnett, 94–95, 96, 98–99

U

unions, labor, 130
United States of America, 52–53, 119,
  127, 131

Untouchables, 61, 67
  See also caste
Upanishads, 63–64

V

Vaiśyas, 60, 62, 63
varna, 60–63, 66–67
vegetarianism, 70
Vimalakīrti, 68, 92–93

W

Weber, Max, 9, 28, 71, 72 65, 82, 98
World War II, 5, 14
world-renouncing:
  Bible and, 79
  caste and, 55–56, 60–62, 64–67, 113
  individualism and, 17, 54, 55, 67–70,
    114
  out-worldliness, 71, 72, 77, 78–79, 115
  sacrifice and, 63
  this-worldly, 71–72
  See also bhikkhus; Buddhism;
    Christianity; Hinduism; man-
    outside-the-world; monasticism;
    *sannyāsīn*s

Y

Yajnavalkya, 64

Z

Zen, 110

© Equinox Publishing Ltd. 2008

Printed in the United States
211674BV00001B/2/P

9 781845 532734